ETHICS

IN AMERICAN LIFE

Keith Goree

Instructor of Applied Ethics
Saint Petersburg Junior College
Saint Petersburg, Florida

South-Western Educational Publishing

I(T)P

International Thomson Publishing

South-Western Educational Publishing is a division of International Thomson Publishing, Inc. The ITP trademark is used under license.

ISBN: 0-538-63489-8

9 10 11 12 13   PR   08 07 06 05

Printed in the United States of America

VP/Editor-in-Chief: Dennis Kokoruda
Managing Editor: Carol Volz
Developmental Editor: Bob Sandman
Acquisitions Editor: Nancy Long
Marketing Manager: Larry Qualls
Production Manager: Carol Sturzenberger
Production Editor: Denise Wheeler
Photo Editor: Devore M. Nixon
Cover Design: Sandy Weinstein
                Tin Box Studio
Photo Illustration: Alan Brown
                Photonics Graphics, Inc.

PREFACE

This preface is addressed primarily to the student. An Introduction to Teachers is included in the Teacher's Manual.

INTRODUCTION TO STUDENTS

A boy in your class returns a wallet that he found, and the money in it, to its owner. Another boy in class is caught cheating on an exam. A girl in your class volunteers several hours of her time every week to help children in a homeless shelter. Another girl lies to her parents about her whereabouts the night before. One employee in a department store figures out a way to help the environment by recycling old boxes. Another employee steals money out of a cash register. Everywhere you look, it seems we are surrounded by questions of ethics.

In ethics we study about what is morally good and bad, right and wrong. We seek to learn what makes actions right or wrong. As you will see, that is a much more complex question than it first seems. Before we begin our study of ethics, however, there are a few important things about this book that you need to know.

ETHICS IN AMERICAN LIFE WILL . . .

- Help you to be more sensitive to the ethical issues around you. Once you learn to recognize ethical issues, you will be amazed at all the places you will see them—at home, at school, in your community, and throughout the nation.

- Help you to learn to appreciate the individual and cultural diversity that is present in American ethics. It sometimes seems frustrating that Americans don't think more alike, but the good news is that we aren't supposed to! How could we, when our experiences and histories are so different? Ethics is not about getting everyone to agree with each other, but listening to, understanding, and respecting ethical points of view that differ from your own.

- Help you to learn to think more clearly, critically, and logically about difficult ethical issues and questions. Carefully thinking through an ethical problem is the first step in finding the best answer.

- Give you the tools necessary to make more mature and responsible ethical decisions—decisions on which you can look back later with pride, rather than regret.

- Help you to develop more confidence in your ethical beliefs and opinions. You will learn to better understand why you believe and act the ways you do. You will also learn to better defend your beliefs when they are questioned by others.

- Help you to raise your own personal ethical standards to new, higher levels. You must choose to raise these standards for yourself. Others can only lend advice, support, and encouragement. This "higher road" is not an easy one, or more people would take it. However, as you grow in moral maturity you will find that people will treat you more as an adult, and less as a child. They will respect and trust you more.

- Assist you as you set sail on what it is hoped will be a life-long search for the best answers to life's problems, the best ethical principles to live by, and, eventually, the good life. Again, it seems easier sometimes just to go with the flow, but in the words of Socrates, "not life, but a good life is to be chiefly valued."

ETHICS IN AMERICAN LIFE WILL NOT . . .

- Provide you with a list of rules and regulations to obey in life. The goal of studying ethics is to learn to make responsible and mature moral decisions for yourself.

- Give you a list of opinions with which you are expected to agree. This is not a book of ethical answers. This book is about the process of making decisions about right and wrong.

- Try to manipulate or control your moral beliefs or opinions. There is no secret agenda here to make you think as your teacher thinks. An important part of ethical maturity is developing your own beliefs and opinions, for your own reasons.

- Force you to share your private beliefs, opinions, feelings, and experiences with others. Your right to privacy will be respected. Whenever questions in this book call for personal information of any kind, you will be reminded that you are free to keep those responses to yourself.

THE ORGANIZATION OF ETHICS IN AMERICAN LIFE

The first four chapters represent the foundations of ethics. In these chapters you will investigate the nature of ethics as well as principles that can be used in making ethical decisions. You will learn about the process of moral development. You will also acquire critical thinking skills that can be useful in finding answers to ethical questions.

Chapters 5 through 12 focus on specific ethical issues. Many of these issues are controversial. All are timely and relevant in America today. In fact, you may be surprised how often you will see the topics you discuss in class on the front page of the newspaper and on the evening news.

Each chapter has three sections. The first, the Focus section, features an activity designed to introduce you to ideas in the chapter. The second section is the text of the chapter, in which concepts and ideas are explained. The third section, Applications, contains exercises and assignments that reinforce the ethical concepts you have learned in the chapter.

TIPS FOR GETTING THE MOST FROM THIS COURSE

- Focus on understanding new concepts and learning to apply them to ethical questions. Simply memorizing definitions won't do you much good. Keep asking yourself, "What does this mean?" and "How can I use this?"

- Stay open-minded to new ideas and different points of view. Someone said that a mind is like a parachute—it only functions properly when it is open. You cannot learn anything as long as you think you already have all the answers.

- Keep holding yourself up to the ethical mirror. Evaluate your own ethical strengths and weaknesses as honestly as you can. If you think of this course simply as new words to be learned and blanks to be filled in, you will miss the most important lessons. On the other hand, if you learn to apply the concepts from this course to the ethical questions of everyday life, you will find yourself making ethical decisions that you can be proud of.

ACKNOWLEDGEMENTS

I thank the following individuals who contributed to the review process for this edition:

Mr. Mike Burns
Lloyd High School
Erlanger, Kentucky

Dr. Al Burr
Burr Educational Enterprises Ltd.
Ballwin, Missouri

Mr. Jack Casey
Executive Scholar
Center on Business Ethics
Bentley College
Quogue, New York

Dr. Harry H. Dresser, Jr.
Gould Academy
Bethel, Maine

Dr. James D. Good
Supervisor, Business Education
St. Louis Public Schools
St. Louis, Missouri

Mr. Jim Hill
Upland High School
Upland, California

Ms. Monica James
Cypress Falls High School
Houston, Texas

Mr. David A. Malaro
St. John's Preparatory School
Danvers, Massachusetts

Professor Al Marcella
Tabor School of Business
Millikin University
Decatur, Illinois

Ms. Brenda Sims Palmer
Lehigh Senior High School
Lehigh, Florida

Professor Rosetta Ross
Interdenominational Theological Center
Atlanta, Georgia

Dr. James B. Sauer
Department of Philosophy
St. Mary's University
San Antonio, Texas

Mr. Scott Schaffer
York University
Toronto, Ontario

Mr. Noel S. Selegzi
The Collegiate School
Hunter College High School
New York, New York

Mr. Peter Shea
Metropolitan State University
Minneapolis, Minnesota

Dr. Jeff Turner
Howard Payne University
Brownwood, Texas

Dr. Leslie F. Weber, Jr.
The Lovett School
Atlanta, Georgia

Keith Goree
Saint Petersburg, Florida

CONTENTS

AN INTRODUCTION TO ETHICS

OBJECTIVES

After completing this chapter, you will be able to:

■ 1. Define ethics.

■ 2. Analyze arguments for and against the existence of the concepts of "right" and "wrong."

■ 3. Evaluate different sources of ethical beliefs.

■ 4. Identify the differences among the standards of ethics, etiquette, and law.

■ Focus

Every day you make decisions about whether actions are right or wrong. (See Illustration 1-1 on page 2.) But how often do you stop to think about *why* you believe a behavior is right or *why* it is wrong? In this chapter you will investigate different answers to that question and begin to discover what ethics is about.

WHAT WOULD YOU DO?

Here are seven questions requiring ethical decisions. Be as honest as you can with yourself. You have the right to keep your moral beliefs private. You are free to share them with your teacher and your classmates if you choose, but it is your choice. No one will force you to do so.

For each situation, answer yes or no (maybe is forbidden) and then explain WHY you would make that choice.

Illustration 1-1

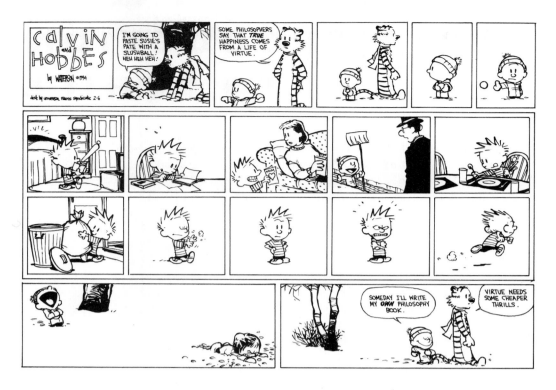

1. Your friend Ellen asks you to tell her parents she was at your house Saturday night. You don't know where she really was. Would you go along with her and be her alibi?

_____

_____

2. You are not doing very well in algebra, and a big test is scheduled for tomorrow. A reliable classmate shows you a copy of the test that he says he found near the school copy machine. Would you use this test to help you get a better grade?

_____

_____

3. Two of your good friends, Jan and Jim, have been dating each other somewhat seriously for the past few months. Jan tells you that she has a date Friday with Tom. She isn't planning to tell Jim about it yet, and she doesn't want you to tell him until she finds out how much she likes Tom. Would you tell Jim anyway?

_____

_____

4. Some chemicals were stolen from the school chemistry lab. A boy who isn't very popular or well-liked has been blamed and is being suspended. You know who really did it. Would you tell a teacher?

_____

_____

5. A close friend, whose grades are about the same as yours, has been accepted at the college you want to attend. She tells you that the secret is to "pad" your application with many more school and community service activities than you really participated in. Would you try her plan?

_____

_____

6. After six games, your school football team is undefeated and might get into the state playoffs. You find out that, without a doubt, two of the stars are using illegal steroids. Would you inform any appropriate authorities?

_____

_____

7. In the school parking lot, you open your car door too forcefully and leave a big scratch on the almost new car next to yours. You know the owner of the other car. Would you admit to her what you did?

_____

_____

> "The sad truth is that most evil is done by people who never make up their minds to be either good or evil." (Hannah Arendt)

ON SECOND THOUGHT

Did the quiz make you think? If you look between the lines, there are several clues in this quiz to help you understand ethics. First, it is clear that many areas of life contain questions concerning right and wrong. Second, people's ethical beliefs are unique. How many of your classmates do you suppose answered every question exactly the same? People base ethical decisions on their personal values and principles, which are developed through individual life experiences. Since everyone has different experiences, it seems reasonable that principles, values, and decisions will vary, too.

Third, notice that there were two parts to your answers. Each part can tell you something about what you will be doing in this study of ethics. There was the "yes or no" section, in which you expressed your ethical decisions. You probably thought about many of your options in terms of their being either _right_ or _wrong,_ or perhaps _good_ or _bad._ Making decisions like these is an important part of the ethical process. However, the most important part of ethics has to do with the "why or why not" section, in which you listed some of your ethical principles.

Ethical principles are general statements of how people should or should not act in most situations. Principles are often the reasons behind our actions, thoughts, and beliefs. One of the most popular ethical principles in America is commonly referred to as The Golden Rule, which says that you should treat others as you would want to be treated. Other popular principles are that you should respect the rights of others, that you should honor your commitments, and that you should take responsibility for your actions. Can you see how one moral judgment could have several ethical principles behind it? Understanding principles like these, and learning to apply them to different ethical situations and issues, is at the heart of what ethics is about.

What is Ethics?

Ethical terms often mean different things to different people, and some individuals claim that these terms have no valid meanings at all. In this section you will be introduced to several foundational definitions, and you will analyze some of those arguments against the existence of moral right and wrong.

BASIC DEFINITIONS

Ethics is the field of philosophy that studies the morality of human conduct. **Morality** refers to that part of human behavior that can be evaluated in terms of right and wrong. Technically speaking, then, *ethics is the study of morality.* However, in practical usage the words *ethical* and *moral* are both used to describe actions that are considered to be good or right, while the words *unethical* and *immoral* are used to describe actions that are considered to be bad or wrong.

DO RIGHT AND WRONG EXIST?

"Great men are they who see that spiritual is stronger than any material force, that thoughts rule the world." (Ralph Waldo Emerson)

Do the concepts of moral right and wrong really exist? Not everyone thinks so. Some argue that the ideas have simply been invented to control people's behavior and limit their freedom. This point of view asserts that right and wrong are really nothing but emotional reactions, religious assumptions, or social agreements. In other words, an action might be morally wrong for you because you believe it to be, but there are no *universal* moral principles, or principles that apply to all people.

After all, these ethical skeptics point out, no two individuals, societies, or religions agree with each other completely on what is right or wrong. If there is a set of moral guidelines for all people, wouldn't it seem logical that we all should agree on what it is? Since we all do not agree, the argument continues, moral right and wrong cannot be anything more than personal opinion. Besides, we live in a scientific age in which the proof for any truth must be based on controlled observation and evidence. If the existence of a universal moral code cannot be proven scientifically, then it must not exist.

CRITICAL THINKING

Do you agree or disagree with these skeptical claims about ethics? Respond to the arguments by turning to page 11 and completing Critical Thinking Exercise 1A.

■ Sources of Ethical Beliefs

Since it seems reasonable to assume that moral right and wrong do exist in some form, where do we get the ethical principles and values that support our beliefs? Some of our principles are the result of lessons taught to us at home, in school, or in religious training. Others are the result of our individual life experiences. For instance, children who grow up in violent neighborhoods probably have different principles than children who grow up more sheltered from danger. We pick up some of our principles from the messages sent by our society through television, music, magazines, and books. In other words, our principles come to us from a variety of sources. However, some of these sources are more influential than others. When asked where we acquire our beliefs about an ethical issue, most of us tend to identify one or more of the following sources. (See Illustration 1-2.)

Illustration 1-2

Culture?   Intuition?   Authority?   Reason?

AUTHORITY

The first potential source of ethical beliefs is **authority**. According to this approach, an action is right or wrong because "someone said so." This way of thinking is often seen in religious ethics, but other moral authorities in history have included monarchs and other kinds of political leaders. When people say, "Stealing is morally wrong because God forbids it," or "Stealing is wrong because the government has made it illegal," they are using the appeal to authority.

CULTURE

Another source of ethical beliefs is **culture**, the idea that the morality of an action depends on the beliefs of one's culture or nation. This approach says that cultures and nations, like individuals, have different values and principles based on their different experiences in history. A belief that works well for one culture

> "The man who never alters his opinions is like standing water, and breeds reptiles of the mind." (William Blake)

may be harmful for another. Because this view assumes that there are no *universal* moral principles, one logical conclusion would be that no nation or culture is able to judge the moral beliefs or actions of another.

INTUITION

A third source of ethical beliefs is **intuition**, which is the idea that principles of right and wrong have been built into your conscience and that you will know what is right by listening to that "little voice" within. This reliance on intuition seems to be very common among Americans. Again, since our consciences seem to vary, this approach implies that there might be no ethical principles or rules that apply to everyone.

REASON

The fourth source of ethical beliefs is **reason**, the idea that consistent, logical thinking should be the primary tool used in making ethical decisions. According to this approach, if stealing is judged to be wrong, then there should be solid arguments and logical principles that back up that judgment. In other words, the arguments against stealing are stronger than the arguments for stealing. With the appeal to reason, an action is not wrong *just* because an authority says so, *just* because it is unpopular within your culture, or *just* because your little voice inside warns you against it. Instead, this approach would suggest that you look open-mindedly at the arguments on both sides of an issue, then use reason carefully to choose the stronger arguments.

CRITICAL THINKING

To evaluate the strengths and weaknesses of these various origins of ethical beliefs, and to better understand their differences, complete Critical Thinking Exercises 1B, 1C, and 1D on pages 12-14.

■ Standards of Behavior

If you lived alone on an island somewhere, the only ethical code you would be concerned about would be your own. But that is not how life really works, is it? The truth is, life is more or less a group project. We experience our lives through families, friendships, neighborhoods, schools, cities, cultures, and countries. Because of that, we have to concern ourselves with the effects of our actions on others and the effects of their actions on us. We can't think about ethics only in individual terms. We are forced to consider standards that might apply to everyone.

A **standard** is an accepted level of behavior to which persons are expected to conform. The level may be set low (a minimum standard), in the middle (an average), or very high (a standard of excellence). Whatever the level, all standards involve some kind of expectation. To say that violating the rights of other

min
avg   standards

ETHICS IN AMERICAN LIFE

people is wrong does not mean that it is wrong for just one person, or even a few people. If it is part of a social standard, then it is assumed that violating rights is wrong for everyone. To be sure, there are ethical issues that are individual and personal, too, but ethics often deals with principles that apply to everyone. People's actions can be evaluated according to many standards, but three of the most common are the standards of etiquette, law, and ethics.

ETIQUETTE

The **standard of etiquette** refers to expectations concerning manners or social graces. Societies and cultures have their own rules of etiquette that their members are expected to meet. Most Americans understand this country's etiquette standards and try to live up to them. Thus, we know to knock before entering someone else's home, and we try to remember to say "please" and "thank you." We take for granted that everyone should understand these rules, even though many of them are not written down anywhere. For example, we don't expect people to smell "daisy-fresh" every minute of every day, but it is understood that there is a certain strength of body odor beyond which they should not go in public. Oddly enough, everyone knows exactly how loud a burp can be before it is considered rude. People who violate these standards of etiquette run the risk of being embarrassed or of being looked down on by others.

In a society as crowded, busy, and stressed as ours, etiquette serves an important function. It reduces social friction and makes it easier for us to live together as a community. But there is an important difference between the standards of etiquette and ethics, and that difference is *seriousness*. The issues covered by the standard of etiquette are not as serious as those in ethics. People hardly ever die due to poor manners, but the ethical standard applies to many life and death issues, such as abortion, euthanasia, war, capital punishment, and AIDS. Even ethical issues that are not associated with death, like censorship, honesty in government, and sexual ethics, still have serious implications.

LAW

The **standard of law** has to do with rules of behavior imposed on people by governments. Like ethics, this legal standard can be serious, too. After all, many laws deal with life and death issues, including rules forbidding murder, drunken driving, drug use, and child abuse. Yet, while legal and ethical standards are both serious, they have an important difference—*validity*. What makes a law valid, or what gives it legal force, is different from that which makes an ethical principle or judgment valid.

CRITICAL THINKING

To better understand what makes a law valid, turn to page 14 and complete Critical Thinking Exercise 1E.

ETHICS

As you may have noted in the previous exercise, the only factor that matters in determining the validity of a law is whether the person who proclaimed it had the authority to do so. With the ethical standard, however, authority is not what matters most. The **standard of ethics** refers to social expectations of people's *moral* behavior. The ethical principles and rules making up this standard are

> "If a man will begin with certainties, he shall end in doubts; but if he will be content to begin with doubts, he shall end in certainties."
> (Sir Francis Bacon)

> "Man's greatness lies in the power of thought." (Blaise Pascal)

Illustration 1-3

	Legally Right and Morally Right	Legally Right but Morally Wrong
Legally Right ▲ (Legal Standard) ▼ Legally Wrong		
	Legally Wrong but Morally Right	Legally Wrong and Morally Wrong

Morally Right ◀   (Ethical Standard)   ▶ Morally Wrong

"Man is the only animal that blushes, or needs to." (Mark Twain)

"The world has achieved brilliance without conscience. Ours is a world of nuclear giants and ethical infants." (General Omar Bradley)

made valid by the reasons and arguments supporting them. Because of this crucial difference, legal standards and moral standards do not always agree. As a result, and as Illustration 1-3 demonstrates, any action can be described in one of four ways:

1. It could be legally right and considered morally right.

2. It could be legally right but considered morally wrong.

3. It could be legally wrong and considered morally right.

4. It could be legally wrong but considered morally wrong.

CRITICAL THINKING

To explore the differences between legal and moral standards, turn to page 15 and complete Critical Thinking Exercise 1-F.

As you can see, people sometimes have to choose between obeying the law and doing what they believe to be morally right. Many people in history have gone to prison, and even to their deaths, rather than violate their ethical beliefs. Another difference is that a legal standard (based on authority) may change as authorities change, but an ethical standard (based on reason) changes only when new information is found that causes people's thinking about the standard to change. Also, a legal standard discourages questioning and challenging, since those actions are often perceived as threats to authority. On the other hand, an ethical standard *requires* the honest questioning and challenging that comes with independent thinking, for that is the only way a society can continue to learn and find better answers.

This section is reserved for your personal experiences, beliefs, and reflections. You will not be expected or required to turn in these responses.

1. List some of the ethical principles and rules that you have adopted for your life. Where did you learn them? Who taught them to you?

ETHICAL PRINCIPLES/RULES   **SOURCE**

a. _____   _____

b. _____   _____

c. _____   _____

d. _____   _____

e. _____   _____

f. _____   _____

g. _____   _____

h. _____   _____

i. _____   _____

j. _____   _____

2. Are there some principles or rules that you have chosen not to adopt for your life, even though someone else wanted you to choose them?

PRINCIPLES/RULES   **WHY NOT CHOSEN**

a. _____   _____

b. _____   _____

c. _____   _____

d. _____   _____

e. _____   _____

f. _____   _____

g. _____   _____

h. _____   _____

3. Can you remember times when you have faced ethical problems and based your decisions on one or more of the following sources of ethical beliefs? Give an example of a situation where you relied on each source.

Authority

_____

_____

Culture

_____

_____

Intuition

_____

_____

Reason

_____

_____

4. Journal.

a. The most important ideas that I learned from this chapter were:

_____

_____

b. Something that this chapter made me think about was:

_____

_____

c. Some ideas I would like to investigate further and learn more about are:

_____

_____

How would you respond to the following arguments? Circle agree or disagree, then write reasons explaining why you answered as you did.

1. **"Unless everyone agrees completely on which actions are 'right' and which actions are 'wrong,' the concepts of right and wrong cannot exist."**

   AGREE   **DISAGREE**

   _____

   _____

2. **"People cannot agree about which actions are right and which actions are wrong."**

   AGREE   **DISAGREE**

   _____

   _____

3. **"Since ethical decisions are based on individual beliefs, we cannot judge each other's actions as being right or wrong."**

   AGREE   **DISAGREE**

   _____

   _____

4. **"Since every society decides for itself what it considers right or wrong, one society can never judge another's actions or moral code."**

   AGREE   **DISAGREE**

   _____

   _____

5. **"If we can't prove scientifically that something exists, then it cannot exist."**

   AGREE   **DISAGREE**

   _____

   _____

Evaluate the sources of ethical beliefs that you have been reading about. List some of the strengths and weaknesses that you see in using each source as a basis for a person's beliefs about right and wrong.

Authority

Strengths   **Weaknesses**

_____   _____

_____   _____

_____   _____

_____   _____

Culture

Strengths   **Weaknesses**

_____   _____

_____   _____

_____   _____

_____   _____

Intuition

Strengths   **Weaknesses**

_____   _____

_____   _____

_____   _____

_____   _____

Reason

Strengths   **Weaknesses**

_____   _____

_____   _____

_____   _____

_____   _____

Think about some of the consequences of following each of the sources of ethical beliefs listed. Answer yes or no in the boxes provided. Be ready to explain your responses.

Critical Thinking Exercise 1C, Page 6

SOURCE	ENCOURAGES QUESTIONING & CHALLENGING?	UNIVERSAL STANDARDS FOR EVERYONE?	INVITES DEBATE OVER ISSUE ITSELF?
AUTHORITY			
CULTURE			
INTUITION			
REASON			

Critical Thinking Exercise 1D, Page 6

Look at the following general moral judgments. In each case, use the appeal to reason to determine why these actions are considered right or wrong. In the first section, give a principle that could be used to back up the judgment. Then, in the second section, tell why you think that principle should be followed.

1. **It is wrong to tell a secret that you promised to keep confidential.**

   a. **Write a principle that could support this statement.**

   _____

   _____

   b. **Why should people follow that principle?**

   _____

   _____

2. **It is right to be willing to defend your country in time of war.**

   a. **Write a principle that could support this statement.**

   _____

   _____

   b. **Why should people follow that principle?**

   _____

   _____

3. It is wrong to discriminate against a person based on his or her race or religion.

   a. Write a principle that could support this statement.

_____

_____

   b. Why should people follow that principle?

_____

_____

4. Write your own moral statement below.

_____

_____

   a. Write a principle that could support this statement.

_____

_____

   b. Why should people follow that principle?

_____

_____

Critical Thinking Exercise 1E, Page 7

Assume that the speed limit on the street outside your school is 35 miles per hour. What makes that a valid law? On the lines below, list factors that might make the law valid, then decide if this factor is true of all valid laws, or only some of them.

POSSIBLE FACTORS	TRUE OF ALL VALID LAWS?
_____	_____
_____	_____
_____	_____
_____	_____
_____	_____

ETHICS IN AMERICAN LIFE

List several actions that could fit into each of the categories discussed in the text. Here are a couple of hints to help you:

1. Only some (not all) people need to consider an action morally right or wrong for it to qualify as an example.

2. Countries, states, and communities have different laws. An action only needs to be legally right or wrong in one place (not everywhere) to qualify as an example.

a. Actions that are legally right and considered morally right:

_____

_____

b. Actions that are legally right but considered morally wrong:

_____

_____

c. Actions that are legally wrong and considered morally wrong:

_____

_____

d. Actions that are legally wrong but considered morally right:

_____

_____

1. You can do a variation of Critical Thinking Exercise 1F by listing policies and rules at your school that you believe fit the different categories given.

a. Actions that are allowed and considered morally right:

_____

_____

b. Actions that are allowed but considered morally wrong by some:

_____

_____

c. Actions that are not allowed and considered morally wrong:

_____

_____

d. Actions that are not allowed but considered morally right by some:

_____

_____

2. In Your Own Words . . .

Rewrite the meaning of each of these words or phrases, but don't use the same words that were used in this chapter. What do they mean *in your own words?*

a. Ethical principle

_____

_____

b. Immoral (or unethical)

_____

_____

c. Moral (or ethical)

_____

_____

d. Moral issue

_____

_____

e. Moral judgment

_____

_____

f. The source of authority

_____

_____

g. The source of culture

_____

_____

h. The source of intuition

_____

_____

i. The source of reason

_____

_____

j. A standard

_____

_____

k. An etiquette standard

_____

_____

l. A legal standard

_____

_____

m. An ethical standard

_____

_____

n. A universal ethical principle

_____

_____

3. Media Scavenger Hunt:

Spend a few days searching in a variety of media sources for stories about ethical issues. Your sources can include newspaper and magazine articles, even advertisements! When you return to class, compile your clippings with those of your classmates and create "ethics collage" posters.

4. List some important ethical issues that you see your society or community wrestling with and debating.

abortion - esp.

iraq - should we be there or not?

smoking ban

3 strikes law

3 of 5 ~police officers~ acquited in Bell shooting in NY
shot @ car 82 times

Euthanasia

government & privacy (tapping phones, etc.)

Hoover moving to Mexico

Immigration Reform

THE DIVERSITY OF AMERICAN ETHICS

OBJECTIVES

After completing this chapter, you will be able to:

- 1. State reasons for America's ethical diversity.
- 2. Explain specific ethical principles based on consequences, virtues, duties, and rights.
- 3. Evaluate the strengths and weaknesses of these principles.
- 4. Apply these principles to moral questions.

■ Focus

Sometimes it seems as if there are as many different opinions about moral right and wrong as there are people. (See Illustration 2-1.) Have you ever wondered why that is so? In this chapter you will investigate some of the reasons behind America's ethical diversity and learn more about some of the various approaches used by people to make moral decisions.

■ Why Do They See It So Differently?

The crowd outside the courthouse was in a frenzy. The trial of a local doctor was finally over. She was charged with second degree murder for helping a terminally ill man kill himself with an overdose of sedatives. The jury had just delivered its verdict: not

Illustration 2-1

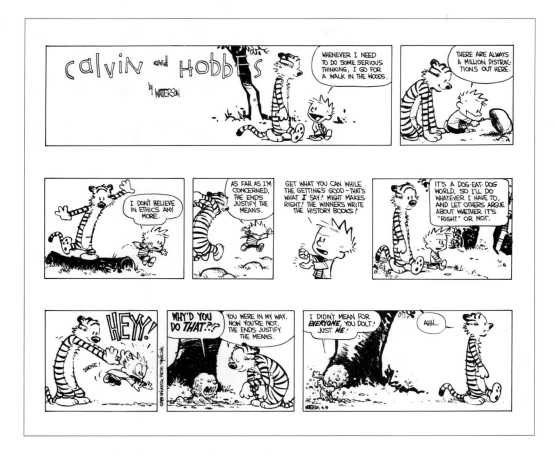

guilty! As the weary doctor struggled to get through the mob of supporters, protesters, and reporters, an angry man in the crowd shouted, "Where's your respect for human life, Doc? The consequences of your actions were that an innocent man was killed! Doesn't the virtue of saving human life mean anything to you doctors anymore?"

Startled, the doctor stopped in her tracks. As the crowd quieted, she said firmly, "I became a doctor because I believe in the virtue of respecting human life. I am aware of the consequences of my actions on this patient, as well as on myself and my family. But my duty as a physician is not only to keep bodies alive, but also to help people improve the quality of their lives. I save lives whenever I can, but compassion is a virtue, too. This patient was suffering terribly and death was inevitable. I believe he had a right to choose to leave this world on his own terms with dignity. I also believe that it was my professional duty to help him."

WHAT DID THEY REALLY SAY?

The four following key words could be used as parts of arguments either for or against the doctor's actions. Find each of these key words in the preceding story and paraphrase the statements in which you find them. Then explain whether you think the doctor's actions were right or wrong and why you think so.

1. Virtue _____

_____

_____

     ETHICS IN AMERICAN LIFE

2. Consequence _____

_____

_____

3. Duty _____

_____

_____

4. Right _____

_____

_____

5. Were the doctor's actions right or wrong? Explain why you think the way you do.

_____

_____

_____

ON SECOND THOUGHT

One of the first things you will probably notice about ethics is that not all people look at ethical issues and questions in the same way. While this is true in most cultures and societies, this diversity is particularly obvious in America. The citizens of this country belong to many different subcultures, distinguished by factors such as race, culture, national origin, and religious affiliation. Each of these subcultures has (or had at one time) its own unique *ethical system,* meaning its own way of deciding which actions are moral and which are immoral. In addition, our ethical beliefs are affected by our experiences in life, our peer groups, and possibly other factors we do not yet understand. When you think about it, it's a wonder we agree on anything at all! But sometimes we do, don't we? There are some ethical answers on which most of us agree, because we share many common ethical principles. In this chapter we will investigate some of these universal principles.

> "Expedients are for the hour, but principles for the ages." (Henry Ward Beecher)

Basing Morality on Consequences

One of the most common ways of considering morality is to think of actions as having good or bad consequences. **Consequences** are the effects or results of what we do. (See Illustration 2-2.) According to this way of looking at ethics, a

Illustration 2-2

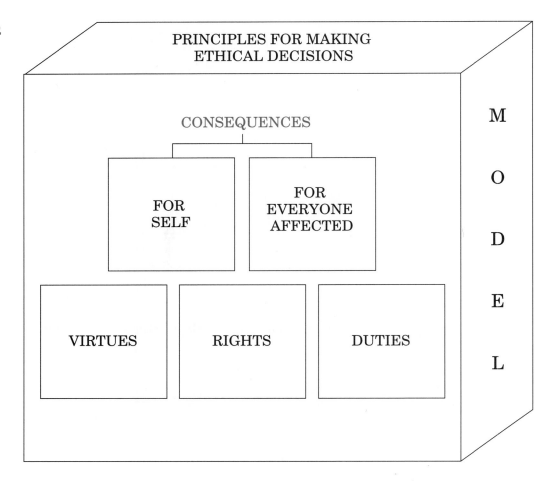

PRINCIPLES FOR MAKING
ETHICAL DECISIONS

M O D E L

CONSEQUENCES

FOR
SELF

FOR
EVERYONE
AFFECTED

VIRTUES

RIGHTS

DUTIES

moral action is one that brings about good consequences, and an immoral action is one that causes bad consequences. Thus, killing another person would usually be considered wrong because it normally leads to bad results. However, those who see ethics from this point of view might argue that when killing another person would have good results it would be the right thing to do. There are two main ethical principles that are part of consequential ethics.

THE EGOISM PRINCIPLE

The first principle claims that you should consider only the effects an action will have on yourself and your interests. The **egoism principle** is the idea that the right thing for a person to do in any situation is the action that best serves that person's own long-term interests. (See Illustration 2-3.) No one else's interests need be considered. If you are deciding whether or not to steal money from the cash register where you work, this principle would lead you to think about the effects the act would have on you. Would it be better for you in the long run to steal the money, or to leave it there? The answer probably depends on how badly you need the money and your estimation of the odds of getting caught. But according to the egoism principle, you do not need to consider the consequences for the owner of the store, your co-workers, or the customers who might now have to pay higher prices. The egoism principle maintains that your only moral obligations are to yourself.

> "Self-interest is but the survival of the animal in us. Humanity only begins for man with self-surrender." (Henri Amiel)

Illustration 2-3

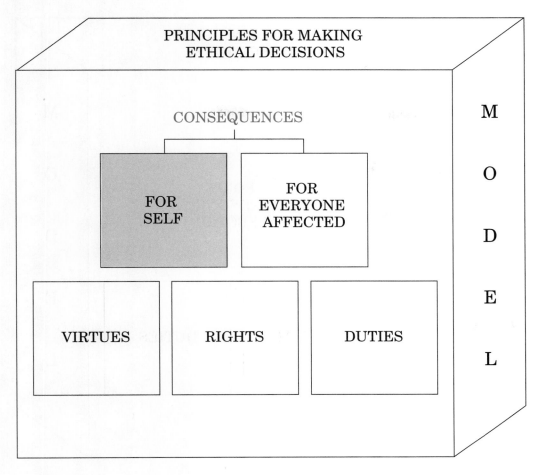

PRINCIPLES FOR MAKING
ETHICAL DECISIONS

CONSEQUENCES

FOR SELF

FOR EVERYONE AFFECTED

VIRTUES

RIGHTS

DUTIES

M O D E L

THE UTILITY PRINCIPLE

The second principle, the **utility principle**, is the idea that the morally right action is the one that produces the best consequences for everyone involved, not just for one individual. (See Illustration 2-4.) Think back to the decision about stealing the money. Using the utility principle would require that you consider the effects that your action will have on everyone: you, the store's owner, your co-workers, the customers, and possibly even your lawyer. In this situation, if stealing produces more *total* good or happiness for everyone than not stealing, then taking the money would be the right thing to do. If not, you should leave it in the drawer.

STRENGTHS AND WEAKNESSES OF CONSEQUENTIAL ETHICS

The strengths of these consequential approaches to ethics are that they are fairly easy to use and they seem very natural to people. After all, it's just common sense to consider the consequences of an action before deciding whether or not to do it. However, these approaches have some serious weaknesses, too. First, both principles require you to accurately predict the consequences of all of your actions. Can you really do that? The consequences of our actions often surprise us. Second, neither approach considers any action to be always right or always wrong. Killing an innocent person can be justified by the egoism principle when doing so is in your long-term best interests. Killing an innocent person can be permitted by the utility principle when doing so produces enough total happiness

"The greatest happiness of the greatest number is the foundation of morals and legislation." (Jeremy Bentham)

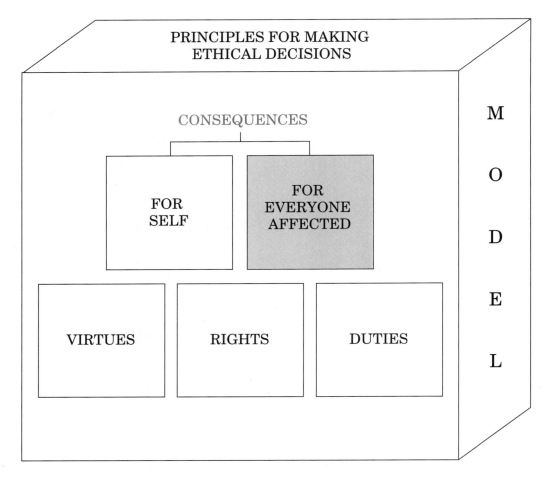

Illustration 2-4

PRINCIPLES FOR MAKING
ETHICAL DECISIONS

CONSEQUENCES

FOR
SELF

FOR
EVERYONE
AFFECTED

VIRTUES

RIGHTS

DUTIES

M
O
D
E
L

for everyone. Although considering the consequences of our actions is clearly a good idea, making sound moral decisions seems to require more.

CRITICAL THINKING

To further consider the strengths and weaknesses of the egoism principle and the utility principle, turn to page 33 and complete Critical Thinking Exercise 2A.

Basing Morality on Virtues

A third ethical principle focuses on the role of ethical virtues. A **virtue** is an ideal character trait that people should try to incorporate in their lives, or a trait commonly found in morally mature people. (See Illustration 2-5.) These traits are considered good in themselves, not good because of their consequences. Examples of ethical virtues could include such ideals as honesty, loyalty, respect, responsibility, self-discipline, compassion, and courage. An action that is consistent with virtues like these is considered to be good or moral. An action that conflicts with such virtues is considered bad or immoral.

ETHICS IN AMERICAN LIFE

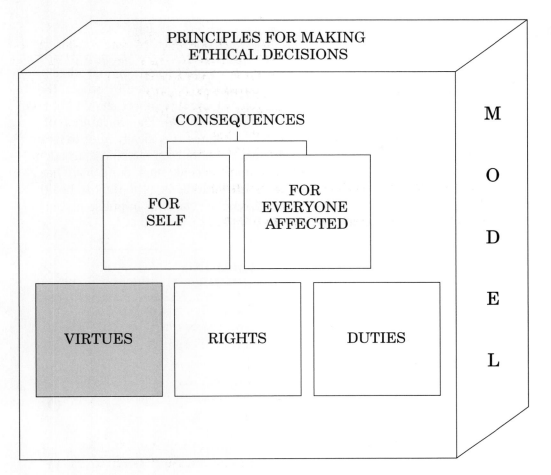

Illustration 2-5

PRINCIPLES FOR MAKING
ETHICAL DECISIONS

CONSEQUENCES

FOR
SELF

FOR
EVERYONE
AFFECTED

VIRTUES

RIGHTS

DUTIES

M
O
D
E
L

THE PRINCIPLE OF VIRTUES

The principle of virtues would judge stealing the money from the cash register to be wrong because doing so conflicts with the ethical virtues of honesty, integrity, and fairness. Whether this particular act of stealing would have good or bad consequences does not matter. The principle of virtues would judge stealing to be *inherently bad*, or bad in itself.

STRENGTHS AND WEAKNESSES OF THE PRINCIPLE OF VIRTUES

A strength of using virtues as a basis for making decisions is that these virtues encourage people to high levels of moral behavior. Some philosophers of ethics, including Plato and Aristotle, have maintained that the key to becoming a morally mature person is acting on these virtues until they become habits. However, this principle also has its weaknesses. One problem is that some actions could promote one virtue while violating another. In addition, when such a conflict exists, people do not always agree on which virtues are most important. Thus, in the case at the beginning of this chapter, the doctor believed that the virtues of compassion and kindness outweighed the virtue of saving human life. Her opponents saw it the other way. When virtues alone are used to find answers to ethical questions, there may be no way to resolve such conflicts.

"Wisdom, compassion and courage— these are the three universally recognized moral qualities of men." (Confucius)

CRITICAL THINKING

To look more deeply into the strengths and weaknesses of using the principle of virtues, complete Critical Thinking Exercise 2B on page 33.

■ Basing Morality on Individual Rights

A third way of considering ethics involves basing moral decisions on individual rights. A **right** refers to how an individual is entitled to be treated by others. (See Illustration 2-6.) For example, your *right to life* implies that others should not take away your life because they owe you the opportunity to live. The Declaration of Independence and the Constitution of the United States specifically refer to many such rights, including the following: life, liberty, the pursuit of happiness, freedom of speech, and the right to have a fair trial. In more recent years, our society has debated whether individuals have the right to die with dignity, the right to health care, the right to an abortion, and the right to smoke cigarettes in public places.

Illustration 2-6

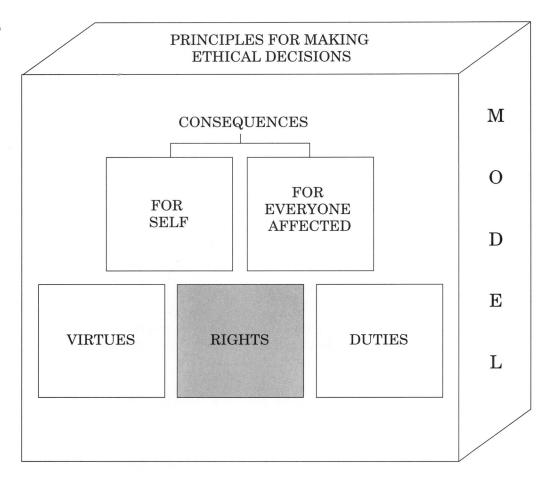

PRINCIPLES FOR MAKING
ETHICAL DECISIONS

CONSEQUENCES

FOR
SELF

FOR
EVERYONE
AFFECTED

VIRTUES   RIGHTS   DUTIES

M O D E L

THE PRINCIPLE OF RIGHTS

According to the principle of rights, an action is considered moral if it respects the rights of others and is considered immoral if it violates anyone's rights. Therefore, stealing from the cash register would be considered wrong because, in taking other people's money, you are violating their property rights. As you saw with the principle of virtues, good or bad consequences are not what makes an action right or wrong. Killing people would nearly always violate their right to life, even if the consequences of killing them were good for you or for a larger group.

STRENGTHS AND WEAKNESSES OF THE PRINCIPLE OF RIGHTS

One strength of the principle of rights is that it gives people a great deal of moral freedom. As long as you don't violate the rights of others, you can do whatever you want. This emphasis on independence and personal freedom is probably why the founders of the United States made rights such an important part of our government and legal system. However, the rights approach has drawbacks, too. One is that people do not always agree on what their rights are. Your seventeen-year-old friend may think that she has the right to stay out all night, but her parents probably disagree. If it were easy to sort out what rights people have, the debates over issues such as abortion, the death penalty, and euthanasia would have been settled long ago.

CRITICAL THINKING

Turn to Critical Thinking Exercise 2C on page 34 and think through some of the other strengths and weaknesses of the principle of rights.

> "Inability to tell good from evil is the greatest worry of man's life." (Cicero)

■ Basing Morality on Duties

The final way of considering ethics that we will discuss in this chapter focuses on moral duties. A moral **duty** is an ethical obligation that one individual has to others. (See Illustration 2-7.) Notice that this definition is the reverse of the one given for a right. In fact, rights and duties can be thought of as opposite sides of the same coin. Your right to life implies that others have a moral duty not to kill you. Your neighbor's right to privacy implies that you have a duty not to read his mail without his permission.

THE PRINCIPLE OF DUTIES

One of the classic explanations of ethical duties came from the German philosopher, Immanuel Kant (1724-1804). He wrote that fulfilling moral duties is the very heart of ethics. Our primary moral duty is to base our actions on good reasoning. Kant believed that good reasoning will lead all people to accept two main ethical principles, universality and respect for persons. The principle of **universality** is the idea that you should act as you would want others to act in the same situation. According to the principle of **respect for persons**, it is always wrong to use other people in ways that harm them for your own benefit. In other words, it is always wrong to take unfair advantage of others for personal gain.

> "Everyone is really responsible to all men and for everything." (Fyodor Dostoyevski)

STRENGTHS AND WEAKNESSES OF THE PRINCIPLE OF DUTIES

A strength of basing ethics on duties is that, like the principle of virtues, this principle motivates people to the highest levels of ethical behavior. Concepts such as universality and respect for persons are extremely challenging to live up to. One the other hand, people do not seem to agree with each other about what their moral duties are. Some people might think that every individual has a moral duty

Illustration 2-7

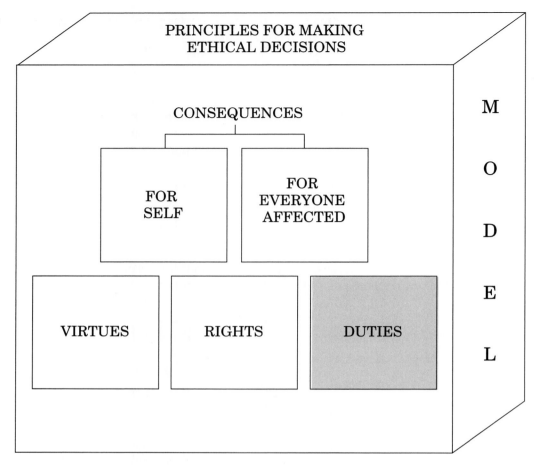

PRINCIPLES FOR MAKING
ETHICAL DECISIONS

CONSEQUENCES

FOR
SELF

FOR
EVERYONE
AFFECTED

VIRTUES

RIGHTS

DUTIES

M
O
D
E
L

to serve in the military. Does the fact that they think so make it an actual duty of yours? How could a society agree on what people's moral duties should be?

CRITICAL THINKING

Complete Critical Thinking Exercise 2D on page 34 by evaluating the duties approach to ethics in more detail. Then practice applying the principles that you have learned so far by working through Critical Thinking Exercise 2E on page 35.

■ Putting It All Together

As you have seen, each of these principles offers some guidance to people facing tough ethical choices, but each one also has weaknesses when used apart from the others. It would seem wise, then, to find a way to use the principles as a group. One way to do this is to take the main idea from each principle and put the ideas together into a model for making ethical decisions. (See Illustration 2-8.)

Illustration 2-8

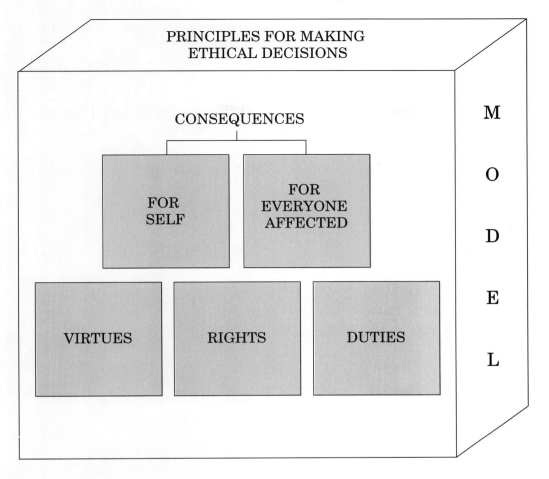

PRINCIPLES FOR MAKING
ETHICAL DECISIONS

CONSEQUENCES

FOR
SELF

FOR
EVERYONE
AFFECTED

VIRTUES

RIGHTS

DUTIES

MODEL

When trying to decide whether a certain action would be right or wrong, you could ask these key questions:

1. Would this action result in more good than bad consequences, or more bad than good?

   a. To me in the long run?

   b. To others who would be affected?

2. How would this action promote or conflict with ethical virtues? Which ones?

3. How would this action affect the rights of other people?

4. Would this action cause me to fulfill or fall short of my moral duties to others? Which duties?

Obviously, a model such as this cannot turn difficult ethical dilemmas into easy answers. There will be situations in which the key questions will not all yield the same answers. There will also be times when one question seems to outweigh all of the others. But the purpose of the model isn't to provide easy answers to all of your questions; it is a tool to help you think carefully through the many implications of your decisions. After all, when people do things that are ethically wrong, it usually isn't because they do not know the right thing to do. More likely, they have chosen to focus on one part of the issue (usually the principle of egoism) and ignore the rest. Thinking through the questions in the model can help

"Courage is the price that life exacts for granting peace." (Amelia Earhart)

you avoid that trap and make decisions that you can look back on with satisfaction rather than regret.

CRITICAL THINKING

Use the model to decide whether Joe should tell his mother about the chemical dump. Complete Critical Thinking Exercise 2F on page 36.

Applications

1. **Think of a time recently when you faced a difficult ethical question or problem. How did you decide what to do?**

   a. **The ethical decision I made had to do with the question or problem of:**

   _____

   _____

   b. **When I look back on how I made my decision, the principles that I relied on the most were:**

   _____

   _____

   c. **If I had it to do over again today, what I would change about how I made my decision is:**

   _____

   _____

2. **List some ethical virtues that you try to live up to:**

   _____

   _____

3. **List some individual rights that are important to you:**

   _____

   _____

4. **List some moral duties that you believe you have an obligation to try to fulfill:**

   _____

   _____

5. Journal.

    a. The most important ideas that I learned from this chapter were:

        _____

        _____

    b. I would like to investigate further and learn more about:

        _____

        _____

    c. I think I could use some of the principles in this chapter to help me make a decision about:

        _____

        _____

List several strengths and weaknesses of relying solely on the principles of egoism and utility when making ethical decisions. Use the text of the chapter to get started, but try to think of some on your own.

Critical Thinking Exercise 2A, Page 24

1. The Egoism Principle

Strengths   **Weaknesses**

_____   _____

_____   _____

_____   _____

2. The Utility Principle

Strengths   **Weaknesses**

_____   _____

_____   _____

_____   _____

Critical Thinking Exercise 2B, Page 25

1. List as many ethical virtues as you can think of. Circle three or four that people you know seem to rely on the most often.

_____

_____

_____

2. List some strengths and weaknesses of relying only on the principle of virtues when facing ethical questions.

Strengths   **Weaknesses**

_____   _____

_____   _____

_____   _____

1. List rights that you think people are entitled to. Circle the ones that people seem to disagree about the most frequently.

_____

_____

_____

_____

2. List some strengths and weaknesses of relying only on the rights principle when making ethical decisions.

Strengths   **Weaknesses**

_____   _____

_____   _____

_____   _____

_____   _____

1. List some moral duties that you believe all people have toward others. Circle the ones that you think people tend to find controversial.

_____

_____

_____

_____

2. List some strengths and weaknesses of relying only on the principle of duties when making ethical decisions.

Strengths   **Weaknesses**

_____   _____

_____   _____

_____   _____

_____   _____

Read the following hypothetical case study. Apply the principles you have learned about in this chapter by answering the questions following the case. Be sure to explain the reasons behind your answers.

CASE STUDY

Joe is a high school senior who plans to be a chemical engineer after college. He also has a well-paying afternoon and weekend job at a local chemical plant. His supervisors there are impressed with his work and have indicated that they plan to offer him a position as a chemical engineer as soon as he has his college degree. They have even set up a scholarship fund to pay some of his college expenses.

One day, while checking on supplies in the warehouse, Joe noticed four workers loading about a dozen old, rusty chemical barrels onto a flatbed truck. The barrels were labeled "HAZARDOUS" and "DANGER." Several of them appeared to be leaking. The workers said that they did not know exactly what was in the barrels, but had been ordered to take them to the dump.

Later, Joe asked his boss, Mr. Peters, for more details. Looking a little uncomfortable, Mr. Peters told Joe that this was a company secret. Mr. Peters made Joe promise never to tell anyone else. Mr. Peters then explained that the company saved thousands of dollars a year by dumping some of its waste chemicals in a lake at the bottom of a nearby, abandoned rock quarry, rather than paying for proper disposal. Joe felt very uncomfortable when he heard this, because he knew that local kids liked to ride their bikes on the hills around the quarry and that the city's water reservoir was only a couple of miles from the quarry.

When Joe mentioned his concerns, Mr. Peters reacted angrily. He told Joe that the money saved through using "the dump" allowed the company to hire high school kids for part-time jobs. He also made it clear that the company wouldn't be interested in hiring any chemical engineers who couldn't keep a company secret.

Joe's mother is an editor at the city newspaper. Should Joe say anything about "the dump" to his mother?

APPLYING THE PRINCIPLES

1. If Joe based his decision *only* on the principle of egoism, how would he make his decision? What action do you think would be in Joe's long-term best interest? Why?

2. **If Joe based his decision *only* on the utility principle, how would he make his decision? What action do you think would have the best overall consequences for everyone? Why?**

_____

_____

3. **If Joe based his decision *only* on moral virtues, what would he think about in making his decision? Which virtues do you think would be the most important? Why?**

_____

_____

4. **If Joe based his decision *only* on individual rights, what would he think about in making his decision? Whose rights are involved in this case? Why?**

_____

_____

5. **If Joe based his decision *only* on moral duties, what would he think about in making his decision? What moral duties do you think he should consider? Why?**

_____

_____

Critical Thinking Exercise 2F, Page 30

Apply the model for ethical decision making to the case study about Joe.

1. **What action would likely result in the best consequences? Why?**

   a. **For Joe in the long run? (egoism)**

   _____

   _____

   b. **For others who would be affected? (utility)**

   _____

   _____

2. What action would best promote *ethical virtues?*

_____

_____

3. What action would best protect the *rights* of others?

_____

_____

4. What action would best help Joe to fulfill his moral *duties* to others?

_____

_____

5. What do you think the model would lead Joe to do? Why?

_____

_____

I. Watch the national and local news on television for several days. Keep track of stories that focus on important ethical issues. Note any references made to the principles of egoism, utility, virtues, duties, and rights. Which principles are mentioned the most often? Why do you think that is so?

_____

_____

_____

_____

_____

2. **Pick one ethical issue that is controversial right now among students at your school. Survey the students, asking for their opinions about the issue and why they think the way they do. Keep track of how many references you hear to the principles of egoism, utility, virtues, duties, and rights. Which ones are the most common? The least? Why do you think this is so?**

_____

_____

_____

_____

_____

3. **Give an example of a recent movie that deals with ethical issues or in which the characters have to make important ethical decisions. Which principles do the characters use? Does the movie portray some principles as working better than others? Do you think they work better in real life?**

_____

_____

_____

_____

4. **Different countries and cultures often have different ways of looking at morality. Do you know any examples of how people in other countries view some ethical issues differently than people in the United States? Do you know any examples of how people in different subcultures within the United States may look at moral issues in different ways?**

_____

_____

_____

_____

_____

THE PROCESS
OF MORAL
DEVELOPMENT

OBJECTIVES

After completing this chapter, you will be able to:

■ 1. Define the concept of moral development.

■ 2. Explain the justice and caring models of moral development.

■ 3. Evaluate strengths and weaknesses of both models.

■ 4. Apply the information from the models to case studies.

■ Focus

You have probably noticed that babies do not seem to have any sense of moral right and wrong. Yet almost all teenagers and adults do. Have you ever wondered how we get this understanding of morality or where it comes from? In this chapter you will explore possible answers to this question. You will also learn strategies for finding out how morally mature you are now and how you can grow in this area in the future.

■ "Hero"

In 1993, musicians Phil Collins and David Crosby co-wrote and recorded the song "Hero." Read the words of the song and think about what they have to say about ethics and deciding between right and wrong.

"It was one of those great stories that you can't put down at night;
The hero knew what he had to do and he wasn't afraid to fight.
The villain goes to jail while the hero goes free;
I wish it were that simple for me.
And the reason that she loved him was the reason I loved him, too;
He never wondered what was right or wrong, he just knew. He just knew.
Shadow and shape mixed together at dawn,
But by the time you catch them simplicity's gone.
So we sort through the pieces, my friends and I,
Searching through the darkness to find the breaks in the sky.

And the reason that she loved him was the reason I loved him, too;
He never wondered what was right or wrong, he just knew. He just knew."

WHAT DO THE LYRICS MEAN?

1. Do you think there really are people who "just know" and don't have to wonder which actions are right and which are wrong? Briefly explain your answer.

_____

_____

2. The lyrics give the impression that they are describing a story. Explain some of the differences between the way characters in books, television shows, and movies are shown making moral decisions and the way people have to make them in the real world.

_____

_____

_____

3. One interpretation of the second stanza is that it describes some of the differences between how young children look at right and wrong versus how morally mature people do. What could the following phrases mean in describing those differences?

a. "Shadow and shape mixed together at dawn"

_____

_____

_____

b. "But by the time you catch them simplicity's gone"

_____

_____

_____

c. "So we sort through the pieces, my friends and I,
   Searching through the darkness to find the breaks in the sky."

_____

_____

_____

ON SECOND THOUGHT

The truth is, making ethical decisions in real life is not clear-cut and simple, is it? Do you know anyone who seems to "just know" what the right thing to do is at all times? At times the answers are obvious, but most of us spend a lot of time "sorting through the pieces" of the ethical gray areas of life. How do we learn to do that? In this chapter you will investigate two models that attempt to answer that question.

> "We cannot learn without pain." (Aristotle)

■ The Justice Model of Moral Development

Justice refers to impartial fairness, or equity. The first model of moral development uses justice as the main criteria in measuring a person's moral maturity. Thus, ethical decisions that are based on self-interest and unfairness would be considered immature.

BACKGROUND

Lawrence Kohlberg was an American psychologist who dedicated his career to understanding human **moral development**, which is the process of growing more ethically mature. He wondered if our ideas about moral right and wrong are based only on what we are taught, or whether some of them are _innate,_ meaning somehow built into us. He wondered whether this ethical maturing process is the same for all humans or whether it varies by individuals, groups, or countries. To find out, Kohlberg studied and interviewed thousands of children from many different nations, cultures, and religious groups.

Typically, Kohlberg would present each child with a case study of a character facing an ethical dilemma. He would ask the child what the character should do in that situation and why. His assumption was that the answer to the _why_ question held the key to understanding the child's moral reasoning, and thus to understanding the child's level of moral development.

KOHLBERG'S STAGES OF MORAL DEVELOPMENT

Kohlberg's research led him to identify six stages of human moral development. One of his most interesting conclusions was that these six stages seem to exist everywhere. Children from varying cultures and religious groups progress through the same sequence of stages of moral reasoning. This finding implies that our sense of morality may not just be limited to what we are taught by others. Like the sequence in physical development of sitting up, crawling, walking, and running, these stages of moral development may be somehow programmed into us.

Stage One—Punishment and Obedience.   In Kohlberg's first stage, right and wrong are perceived in terms of the physical consequences of particular actions. (See Illustration 3-1.) Actions that lead to pleasant consequences are considered good, and those leading to unpleasant consequences are considered bad. Most children learn early in life that disobedience to authority figures (parents) leads to punishment (unpleasant), while obedience leads to praise (pleasant). Soon morality comes to be thought of in terms of obedience to authority and avoidance of punishment.

Illustration 3-1

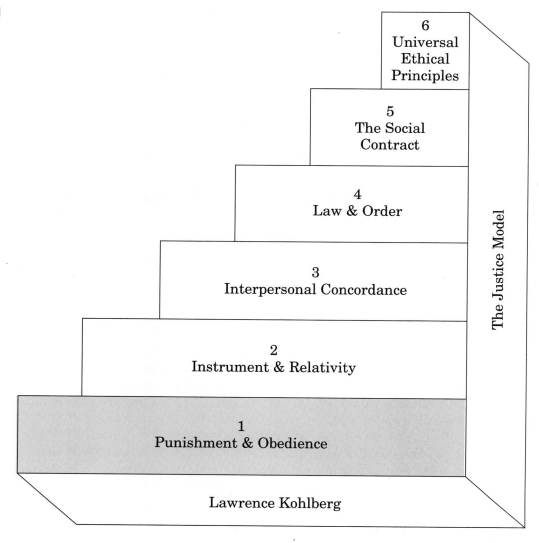

6
Universal Ethical Principles

5
The Social Contract

4
Law & Order

3
Interpersonal Concordance

2
Instrument & Relativity

1
Punishment & Obedience

The Justice Model

Lawrence Kohlberg

Many children understand that hurting others is wrong, but give different reasons when asked why. Typically, children in stage one think of this action as wrong because their parents have told them not to do it, and because those who hurt others get punished. Notice that self-centeredness is at the heart of this way of reasoning. Children in this stage do not understand that other people have feelings and needs like their own and, therefore, are not capable of sympathy or compassion. The only motivating force is the avoidance of punishment for themselves.

Stage Two—Instrument and Relativity.   A child in Kohlberg's second stage has a more realistic view of others. (See Illustration 3-2.) Now other people are seen as having feelings and needs like the child does, but the child is still motivated by self-centeredness. These children think of a right action as one that meets their needs and desires. In other words, morally right actions are the tools (instruments) used to meet personal needs. Therefore, stage two children can be manipulative, using the feelings and needs of others to get what they want. Morality is seen as relative, meaning that it changes according to different situations.

For example, consider a young girl whose room is a mess. Her parents are expecting company soon and are anxious about what the visitors will think if the house doesn't look neat and clean. In stage two, avoiding punishment is less likely

Illustration 3-2

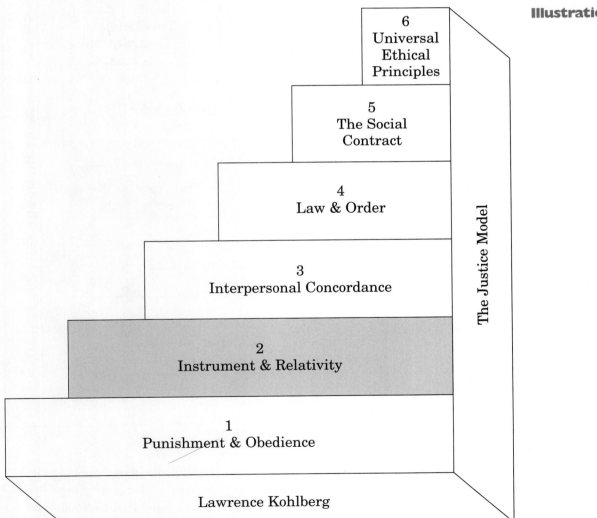

6
Universal
Ethical
Principles

5
The Social
Contract

4
Law & Order

3
Interpersonal Concordance

2
Instrument & Relativity

1
Punishment & Obedience

The Justice Model

Lawrence Kohlberg

to be the reason the girl would clean up her room. She is more likely to notice the stress and tension that her parents are feeling and try to make a bargain, such as cleaning her room in exchange for money or some other reward.

Stage Three—Interpersonal Concordance.

In Kohlberg's third stage, individuals feel a strong need to be liked, accepted, and thought well of by others. (See Illustration 3-3.) The word *concordance* means agreement or harmony. So morally right actions are thought of as those that gain such social approval. Wrong actions are those that bring social condemnation, embarrassment, or rejection. Thus, people in stage three are strongly influenced by peer pressure. The peer group may even replace parents as the primary moral authority. After all, the peer group decides which actions lead to social approval and which ones lead to disapproval.

Illustration 3-3

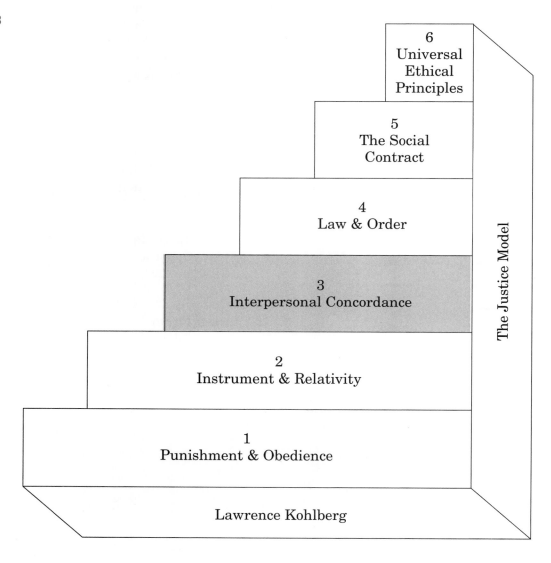

to be the reason the girl would clean up her room. She is more likely to notice the stress and tension that her parents are feeling and try to make a bargain, such as cleaning her room in exchange for money or some other reward.

6
Universal Ethical Principles

5
The Social Contract

4
Law & Order

3
Interpersonal Concordance

2
Instrument & Relativity

1
Punishment & Obedience

Lawrence Kohlberg

The Justice Model

Consider the not unusual case of a 14-year-old boy who starts smoking cigarettes, drinking beer, or experimenting with drugs because his peer group encourages him to. Stage three reasoning leads him to think that these actions are right because of the way the group treats him when he does what's expected.

Unlike stage one and stage two children, he is now willing to sacrifice his own physical self-interest to please the group and gain its approval.

Stage Four—Law and Order. People in Kohlberg's fourth stage have developed a more mature view of the world. (See Illustration 3-4.) The world is now seen as being much bigger than their individual peer groups. Stage four people understand that they are part of a larger community with others, and they feel a moral duty to maintain the order and stability of that community. An action that promotes the harmony and smooth functioning of society is seen as right. An action that interferes with this social order is seen as wrong. As a result, individuals in stage four have a strong sense of citizenship, duty, responsibility, and obedience to the laws of the land.

Illustration 3-4

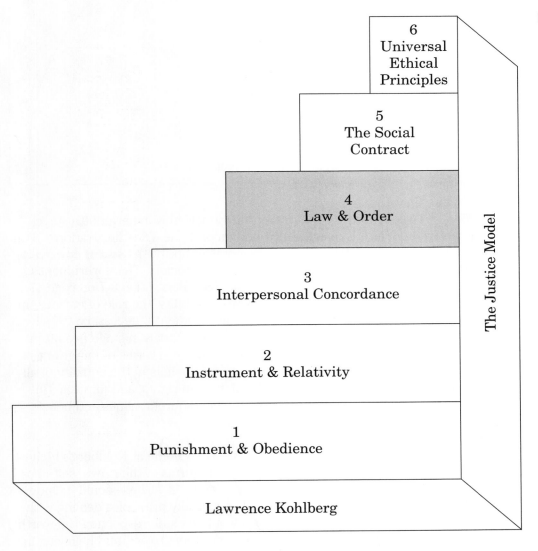

While reasoning at this stage is at a higher level than at the previous stages, it does have a flaw. People in stage four sometimes think of the government as the ultimate moral authority. They define the role of a citizen as obeying that authority. (See Illustration 3-5.) Therefore, these individuals may lack the ability to understand the differences between just and unjust laws. They may conclude that if an action is legally right, it must be morally right as well. As in stage three, the emphasis is on conformity, but now the conformity is to the laws made by government, not just the will of the peer group. Stage four reasoning makes it difficult for a person to understand the need to challenge abuses of authority or to protest unfair laws.

Illustration 3-5

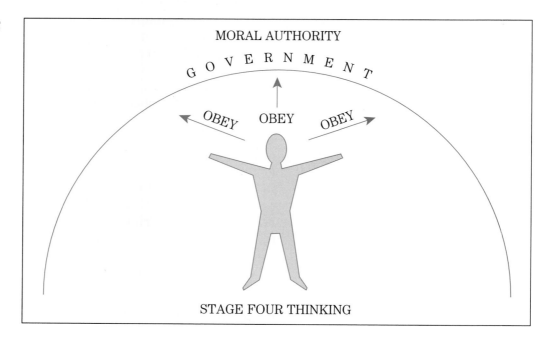

MORAL AUTHORITY

GOVERNMENT

OBEY   OBEY   OBEY

STAGE FOUR THINKING

> "Never do anything against conscience, even if the state demands it." (Albert Einstein)

Stage Five—The Social Contract.   Individuals in Kohlberg's fifth stage view the government as a legal authority, not a moral one. (See Illustration 3-6 on page 47.) They believe that there is a higher moral authority, the **social contract**, which represents the deepest values and beliefs of a society. The government's role is now seen as serving the will of the people. (See Illustration 3-7 on page 47.) When the government fails to live up to that responsibility, the role of citizenship is to question, challenge, and even change the government if necessary.

Because they reason about ethics in this way, individuals in stage five often take on the role of being protesters. They view morality in terms of important social values. In America, these values might include beliefs in the equality of all people, the dignity and worth of the individual, human rights, and fairness. But notice that other societies and cultures would have different values and beliefs and, therefore, would have different social contracts.

> "Right and wrong exist in the nature of things. Things are not right because they are commanded, nor wrong because they are prohibited." (R. G. Ingersoll)

Stage Six—Universal Ethical Principles.   People at Kohlberg's highest level of moral development view right and wrong in terms of their own, self-chosen, universal principles. (See Illustration 3-8 on page 48.) These could include some of the principles discussed in Chapter 2, especially principles dealing with justice or fairness to others. These principles would include respecting the worth and value of human life, acting as you would want others to act, and believing in the importance of individual rights. People in stage five could follow these principles also, but only if the principles were part of their society's social contract. People in stage six would rely on these principles no matter what kind of society they found themselves in.

Kohlberg believed that very few people ever reach this final stage of moral development. People in this stage feel compelled by personal ethical principles to rise above the values and beliefs of their societies. (See Illustration 3-9 on page

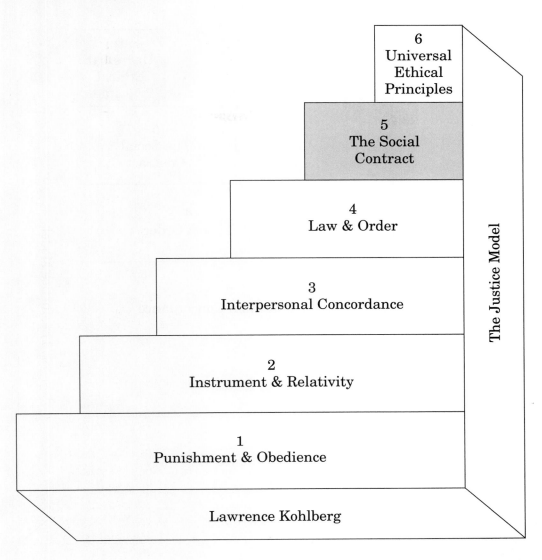

Illustration 3-6

6
Universal
Ethical
Principles

5
The Social
Contract

4
Law & Order

3
Interpersonal Concordance

2
Instrument & Relativity

1
Punishment & Obedience

The Justice Model

Lawrence Kohlberg

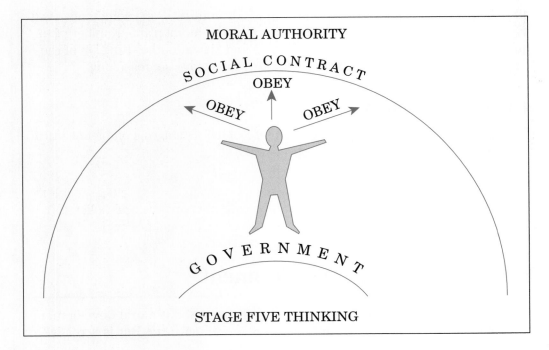

Illustration 3-7

MORAL AUTHORITY

SOCIAL CONTRACT

OBEY

OBEY   OBEY

GOVERNMENT

STAGE FIVE THINKING

Illustration 3-8

```
                                    ┌──────────┐
                                    │    6     │
                                    │Universal │
                                    │ Ethical  │
                                    │Principles│
                              ┌─────┴──────────┤
                              │       5        │
                              │  The Social    │
                              │  Contract      │
                        ┌─────┴────────────────┤
                        │        4             │
                        │   Law & Order        │
                  ┌─────┴──────────────────────┤
                  │          3                 │
                  │Interpersonal Concordance   │
            ┌─────┴────────────────────────────┤
            │            2                     │
            │  Instrument & Relativity         │
      ┌─────┴──────────────────────────────────┤
      │              1                         │
      │   Punishment & Obedience               │
┌─────┴────────────────────────────────────────┤
│              Lawrence Kohlberg                │
└───────────────────────────────────────────────┘
```

The Justice Model

49.) They are willing to sacrifice their own needs, interests, and sometimes even their lives to try to pull their societies up to a higher moral plane. Kohlberg frequently mentioned Mahatma Gandhi of India and Martin Luther King, Jr. of the United States as examples of people demonstrating stage six reasoning.

CRITICAL THINKING

To better understand and remember each of Kohlberg's stages, complete Critical Thinking Exercises 3A and 3B on pages 54-55.

■ The Caring Model of Moral Development

Lawrence Kohlberg's theory answers our questions about moral development if justice is the only standard for measuring moral maturity. But is it really?

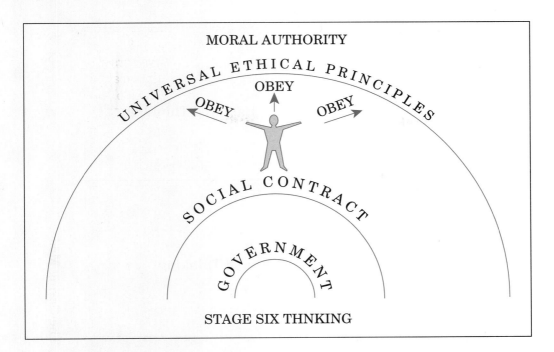

Illustration 3-9

MORAL AUTHORITY

UNIVERSAL ETHICAL PRINCIPLES

OBEY

OBEY

OBEY

SOCIAL CONTRACT

GOVERNMENT

STAGE SIX THNKING

The second theory we will consider uses the concept of caring as its primary standard.

BACKGROUND

While Kohlberg's justice model has been praised as an important first step in our understanding of the process of moral development, it has also received criticism. The strongest criticism so far has come from feminist philosophers. They claim that his model may describe male moral development, but does not apply as well to females. One of this group's most influential spokespersons has been Carol Gilligan. She has created a competing model based on what she believes to be at the heart of how women view ethics, the concept of *caring*.

GILLIGAN'S STEPS IN MORAL DEVELOPMENT

Since Carol Gilligan uses a different standard for measuring moral maturity, it is not surprising that the stages or steps in her theory differ also. Thus, her approach views moral development as a three-step process, with each step defined by how we relate to other people.

Step One—Self-Centeredness.   The first step in the caring model is characterized by self-interest. (See Illustration 3-10.) People at this level care about meeting only their own needs and interests, at the expense of others if necessary. This attitude is usually expressed in acts of selfishness, a lack of concern for others, and in actions that exploit or manipulate others for personal gain.

Step Two—Others-Centeredness.   People at Gilligan's second step feel obligated to ignore their own needs and interests to meet the needs of others. (See Illustration 3-11 on page 51.) In other words, the pendulum has now swung from being self-centered at the expense of others to being others-centered at the

> "Education makes people easy to lead, but difficult to drive; easy to govern, but impossible to enslave." (Henry Potter)

Illustration

3-10

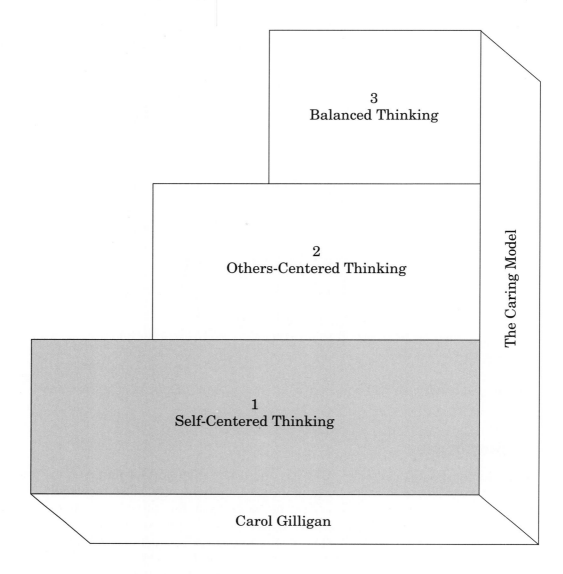

3
Balanced Thinking

2
Others-Centered Thinking

1
Self-Centered Thinking

The Caring Model

Carol Gilligan

expense of oneself. Sometimes this attitude is referred to as the *martyr syndrome*. This is the mistaken belief that seeing yourself as a "good person" requires having to sacrifice yourself or your needs for others.

People at this level often feel guilty when they do something nice for themselves. They don't seem to think that they deserve it. However, Gilligan's point is that people must understand that moral maturity is based on more than self-denial before they can move on to the third and final step.

Step Three—Balancing Needs.   This third step in the caring model is characterized by a sense of balance and flexibility. (See Illustration 3-12 on page 52.) According to Gilligan, morally mature people understand that living a complete life means finding ways to meet both their own needs and interests and those of other people who are close to them. Such people understand that they do not have to feel guilty for trying to meet their own needs. They understand ethics not in terms of caring for me *or* them, but caring for me *and* them.

Illustration
3-11

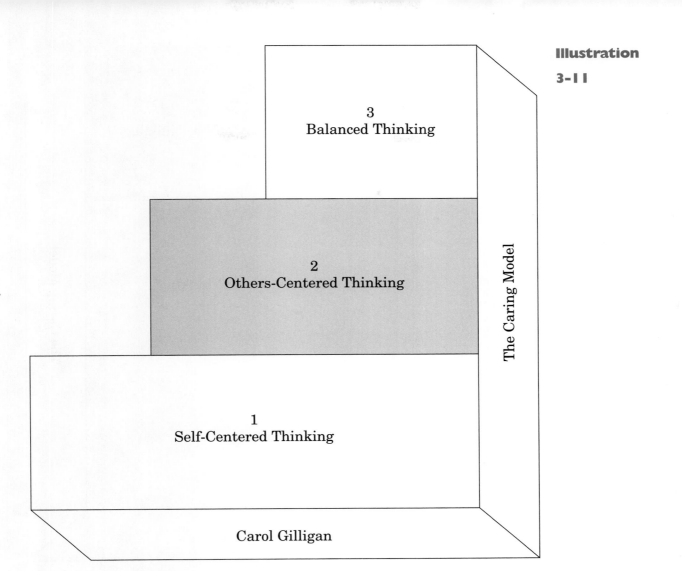

3
Balanced Thinking

2
Others-Centered Thinking

The Caring Model

1
Self-Centered Thinking

Carol Gilligan

■ One Final Note

Almost all great discoveries begin with a great question. Kohlberg's original question—Where do people get a sense of right and wrong?—is an important key to understanding how we can grow to higher levels of moral behavior. It is too early to tell whether the answers Kohlberg and Gilligan found will hold up over time. Other models will surely come along to challenge them. What is most important is that we look honestly and critically at our individual attitudes, beliefs, and actions. Moral growth comes from affirming our strengths and understanding our weaknesses.

Illustration

3-12

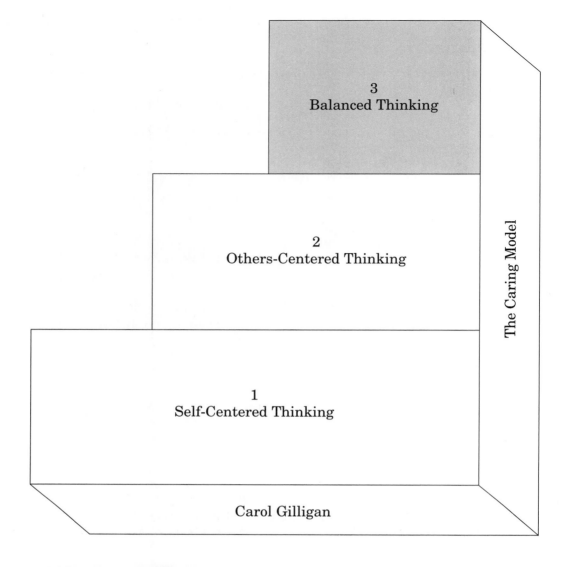

3
Balanced Thinking

2
Others-Centered Thinking

1
Self-Centered Thinking

The Caring Model

Carol Gilligan

CRITICAL THINKING

To help you remember each of the steps in the caring model of moral development, complete Critical Thinking Exercise 3C on page 57. Then to get a better understanding of the practical differences between the justice and caring models, go on to Critical Thinking Exercises 3D and 3E (pages 58-60).

Remember, this section is designed to encourage personal reflection. You will not be asked to share these answers with others.

1. In the *justice model* of moral development, which stage do you see yourself at now? Explain why you think so.

_____

_____

_____

_____

2. In the *caring model* of moral development, which step do you see yourself at now? Explain why you think so.

_____

_____

_____

_____

3. Which of the two models of moral development seems to fit your own life and experiences more closely? In other words, which model do you identify with more? Why?

_____

_____

_____

_____

4. Journal

a. The most important ideas that I learned in this chapter were:

_____

_____

_____

_____

b. Something that this chapter made me think about was:

_____

_____

_____

_____

c. Some ideas that I would like to find out more about are:

_____

_____

_____

_____

d. One thing that I could do to help me grow in moral development is:

_____

_____

_____

_____

Based on each of the stages of the justice model of moral development, give examples of how people might decide what is right or wrong. These examples could either be made up or drawn from your own experiences.

Critical Thinking Exercise 3A, Page 48

1. Stage One—Punishment and Obedience

_____

_____

_____

2. Stage Two—Instrument and Relativity

_____

_____

_____

3. Stage Three—Interpersonal Concordance

_____

_____

_____

3. Stage Four—Law and Order

_____

_____

_____

5. Stage Five—The Social Contract

_____

_____

_____

6. Stage Six—Universal Ethical Principles

_____

_____

_____

Last Saturday, Lee was arrested for trespassing during a protest rally at "Nukes-R-Us," a plant that manufactures parts for atomic weapons and sells them to terrorists. During his interrogation, the police were trying to determine which stage of moral development Lee was operating from, but he kept changing his story. You can help by identifying the correct stage of the justice model for each of his statements.

1. **"This business is violating every principle that our country stands for! The government is wrong to allow companies like this to exist. We are going to stand up for what America believes in and make them change the policy!"**

   Stage _____ **Because** _____

   _____

2. **"I'm really sorry about what happened, but it's not my fault. Some of these protesters are vicious and dangerous. I was afraid they would hurt me if I didn't go along with them."**

   Stage _____ **Because** _____

   _____

3. **"Look, all of my friends belong to this protest group. I couldn't let them down. If I hadn't climbed the fence with them, they would think I was a coward and might not like me anymore."**

   Stage _____ **Because** _____

   _____

4. **"To be honest, I'm not one of the protest group. They paid a bunch of us $50 each if we would make the crowd look bigger for the television cameras. I'll be glad to testify against them if you will drop the charges against me and pay me a little something for my trouble."**

   Stage _____ **Because** _____

   _____

5. **"I cannot stand by silently while a company violates important principles that I believe in deeply. Human life is at stake. Arrest me if you have to, but I have to stand by my principles."**

   Stage _____ **Because** _____

   _____

6. "I'm really an undercover police officer, not a protester. I was spying on the group. Personally, I believe that every law is a good law and that anyone who breaks a law on purpose has done something morally wrong. Book 'em!"

Stage _____ Because _____

_____

Critical Thinking Exercise 3C, Page 52

Based on each of the stages of the caring model of moral development, give examples of how people might decide what is right or wrong. These examples could either be made up or drawn from your own experiences.

1. Step One—Self-Centeredness

_____

_____

_____

_____

2. Step Two—Others-Centeredness

_____

_____

_____

_____

3. Step Three—Balancing Needs

_____

_____

_____

_____

On the spaces below list what you think are the best ideas and biggest weaknesses in each of the models of moral development presented in this chapter.

THE JUSTICE MODEL

Best Ideas:

_____

_____

_____

_____

Biggest Weaknesses:

_____

_____

_____

_____

THE CARING MODEL

Best Ideas:

_____

_____

_____

_____

Biggest Weaknesses:

_____

_____

_____

_____

Read the following case study carefully and then explain how you think Juanita would reason about her ethical dilemma at each stage or step of each model of moral development. Remember, it is how a person reasons, not just what he or she does, that determines his or her level of moral development.

CASE STUDY

Juanita is a senior, only four weeks away from graduation ceremonies at Smallburg High School. She applied to attend a state university in a nearby city and was told that she will be accepted upon graduation from high school. The problem is that, between her part-time job, playing on the basketball team, and being busy in several clubs, Juanita has fallen behind in her schoolwork. It is now dawning on her that she may not pass enough classes to graduate this spring. Attending summer school is an option, but then her family couldn't go on its annual summer trip to Puerto Rico. Juanita doesn't think she could stand it if the whole family missed the trip because of her.

Juanita has figured out that she will only have enough credits to graduate if she passes her senior composition class. To pass, she has to make an "A" on the class research paper that is due in two days. The problem is that she has not yet picked a topic or started her research. She has been too busy catching up in her other classes. It's panic time.

Alan is a neighbor and friend who graduated from Smallburg last year. He tells Juanita that he had the same teacher last year. Alan kept his "A" research paper. He offers to sell it to her for $20. It turns out that Alan bought it for $15 from a cousin who wrote it for a college class.

How would Juanita reason through her decision according to each model of moral development? What do you think she would do at each stage or step?

THE JUSTICE MODEL

Stage One — _____

_____

_____

Stage Two — _____

_____

_____

Stage Three — _____

_____

_____

Stage Four — _____

_____

_____

Stage Five — _____

_____

_____

Stage Six — _____

_____

_____

THE CARING MODEL

Step One — _____

_____

_____

Step Two — _____

_____

_____

Step Three — _____

_____

_____

Reinforcement Exercises

I. **List some of the people whose ethical character and integrity you most look up to and admire. What it is you see in each person that you would most like to develop in your life?**

Persons   I Wish I Saw More of These Qualities in My Life

a. _____

b. _____

c. _____

d. _____

e. _____

2. **Do you think the differences in the justice model and the caring model are really just the differences between how males and females think? Do you think there might be another explanation? Explain why you think the way you do.**

_____

_____

_____

3. **Look for newspaper or magazine articles in which people talk about their ethical or unethical actions. Look for clues as to the possible levels of moral development of the persons in the articles. Bring the articles in for class discussion.**

_____

_____

_____

4. **List several movies or television shows that you have seen recently. At what stages or steps of moral development were the villains? The heroes? Did any characters show changes in moral maturity during the story? What caused the changes?**

_____

_____

_____

5. **In Your Own Words—Explain the main idea in each stage or step or moral development *in your own words*. What do they mean to you?**

THE JUSTICE MODEL

Stage One — _____

_____

_____

Stage Two — _____

_____

_____

Stage Three — _____

_____

_____

Stage Four — _____

_____

_____

Stage Five — _____

_____

_____

Stage Six — _____

_____

_____

THE CARING MODEL

Step One — _____

_____

_____

Step Two — _____

_____

Step Three — _____

_____

_____

CRITICAL THINKING IN ETHICS

OBJECTIVES

After completing this chapter, you will be able to:

- 1. Describe common fallacies in reasoning.

- 2. Identify common fallacies used in logically flawed arguments.

- 3. Explain the steps involved in critical thinking about ethical issues.

- 4. Apply these steps in critical thinking to find answers to ethical questions.

■ Focus

As you have seen in earlier chapters, people decide on their opinions and beliefs in a wide variety of ways. One of the most effective ways is through the use of critical thinking skills. (See Illustration 4-1.) **Critical thinking** is a problem-solving process based on the use of reason, creativity, and consistent thinking. The word *critical* does not refer to criticizing or ridiculing other people. Instead, it is the practice of thoughtfully examining ideas and assumptions, whether held by others or yourself. In this chapter you will learn how to identify and avoid fallacies, which are stumbling blocks to critical thinking. You will also learn how to take the skills you developed in earlier chapters and put them together into a system for finding your own answers to ethical questions.

Illustration 4-1

FRANK & ERNEST® by Bob Thaves

How Do I Decide What To Think?

Briefly write about a recent occasion where you were listening to people argue about a controversial issue or question. Write down any emotions that you remember experiencing (confusion, frustration, etc.). Then explain which view you decided to agree with and why. (Whether you share your answer with others is up to you.)

_____

_____

_____

Fallacies in Ethical Reasoning

The desire to have others agree with our opinions seems to be a part of human nature. So a discussion with a friend over a difference of opinion usually involves each of you sharing and arguing for your own points of view. However, your main goal as a critical thinker is not so much to win arguments as it is to find the best answers you can to life's questions and problems. To achieve this, you will need to acknowledge the strengths in your friend's arguments and admit any weaknesses in your own. If your friend's arguments are stronger than yours, you haven't lost a contest; you've just learned something new. Unfortunately, at times our pride gets in the way of our learning. We fear that if we lose an argument we might appear to be weak. We stop looking for the best possible answers and we start trying to win the argument at all costs. In so doing, we sometimes resort to the use of fallacies.

WHAT ARE FALLACIES AND WHY SHOULD WE AVOID THEM?

Fallacies are inappropriate or deceptive arguments. Ideally, our arguments should appeal to other people's intellects. Fallacies, however, are aimed more at people's emotions. Fallacies are used to manipulate or trick others into agreeing with us. We may win some arguments, but we are not likely to find the best answers to our questions. Therefore, critical thinking in ethics includes trying to avoid the use of fallacies in our arguments and noticing fallacies present in arguments made by others. To do this we first need to understand what some of those fallacies are. The following are twelve of the most commonly used fallacies, the *Dirty Dozen* of logical thinking. (See Illustration 4-2.)

Illustration 4-2

False Appeal to Popularity

False Appeal to Authority

Inconsistency

Provincialism

Two-Wrongs-Make-a-Right

Questionable Claim

Fallacies: The Dirty Dozen

Either/Or

Slippery Slope

Is/Ought

Post Hoc

Red Herring

Hasty Generalization

INCONSISTENCY

Inconsistency is the fallacy of contradicting ourselves in words or actions without being able to explain the changes. It is the error of either saying one thing while doing the opposite or of saying two things that contradict each other. For example, a father might regularly lecture his child about the importance of honesty, but act dishonestly himself. Or a girl could tell her Friday night date that she will love only him forever, and then say the same words to a different boy on Saturday.

TWO-WRONGS-MAKE-A-RIGHT

Two-wrongs-make-a-right is the fallacy of defending something that you did wrong by pointing out that someone else did it, too. A young child, about to be punished for coloring on a wall, protests, "Well, Susie did it first!" And what do people often say (or at least think) when a police officer pulls them over for driving too fast? "Yes, officer, I was going over the speed limit. But you should have seen that guy that just passed me! He was really flying!" Obviously, our wrong actions do not become acceptable just because other people do them too.

EITHER/OR

Either/or is the fallacy of making it appear that there are only two possible sides to an issue, one good and one bad. This fallacy is an attempt to make other people think that they are in a logical trap when, in fact, the trap does not exist. A boy might say to his girlfriend, "Either have sex with me or you don't really love me." Making her feel trapped is an attempt to manipulate her into doing something that she is not ready for. In reality, she may love him deeply and still want to save sexual intercourse until they are married. Another example might be of a friend at school who says, "Either do drugs with us or you can't be cool." These are not really the only two choices.

"We only think when we are confronted with a problem." (John Dewey)

"When you know a thing, to hold that you know it; and when you do not know a thing, to hold that you do not know it: this is knowledge." (Confucius)

IS/OUGHT

Is/ought is the fallacy of stating that, because things are a certain way now, that must be how they should be. Whatever *is* now *ought* always to be that way, so don't change a thing. This fallacy is often used by people who fear change. A famous example of the is/ought fallacy was used to warn against the invention of the airplane. Skeptics said, "If people were meant to fly, they'd have wings." In other words, "People are earthbound now, so that must be how we should remain." Today you can still hear similar arguments used against new forms of technology from increasing experimentation in genetics to the increasing role of computers in society. Some people see change as frightening and find security in keeping things the way they are.

RED HERRING

Red herring is the fallacy of using an unrelated idea in an argument to distract your opponent. It is said that the name of this fallacy came from a once-common practice in English fox hunting. To get the hounds to stop chasing the fox, the hunters would drag a dead fish across the fox's trail. The dogs, charging down the path, would be diverted by the stronger, more interesting scent. The red herring fallacy accomplishes the same goal by using interesting but irrelevant arguments. Can you find the red herring in the following example? It occurred in a debate over whether more laws are needed to protect the environment. "Our planet has serious environmental problems, and, yes, some of Al Gore's environmental ideas make sense. But his wife, Tipper, was one of the leaders in the movement to put parental warning labels on some music albums. Don't you think that's a violation of free speech?"

HASTY GENERALIZATION

Hasty generalization is the fallacy of assuming that most members of a group share a common characteristic, when this assumption is actually based on only a few observations. For example, because two Norwegians spoke harshly to Carla this week, she wrongly assumed that Norwegians as a group are irritable people. Many of the unfair stereotypes and prejudices we have about other groups of people are based on hasty generalizations. These stereotypes often start with our being taught a faulty belief about some other group. Perhaps Carla has grown up hearing that Norwegians are irritable. Then, when she sees a few people from the group act that way, her belief gets reinforced. As a result, people come to believe such stereotypes are true, based on a few examples.

POST HOC

Post hoc is the fallacy of assuming that, because two events happened in a short period of time, the first action must have caused the second one. Our minds interpret events this way to make sense of what we see around us. So when we see events that occur one after the other, our minds sometimes assume that one caused the other. But this assumption is not always accurate and can lead to some funny mistakes. Many superstitions and myths result from post hoc fallacies. For example, "A black cat crossed my path on Tuesday, then on Wednesday I was hit by a bus. That proves black cats are bad luck!" Wouldn't you like to know what happened to the person who started the superstition that walking under ladders causes bad luck? Sometimes one event or action does cause another, but not always. Many times, what looks like a cause is really a coincidence.

SLIPPERY SLOPE

The **slippery slope** fallacy is an attempt to frighten others into rejecting an idea by trying to show that accepting it would start a chain reaction of terrible events. Usually this chain reaction involves a series of steps that keep getting worse and worse. At the end of this chain reaction is usually a terrifying or ridiculous consequence that no sane person would want. Consider the following example of a slippery slope, used to explain why a law banning assault rifles should not be passed. Would passing the law automatically lead to the final result?

"Sure, all the government says it wants to do now is to ban deadly assault rifles. But the next thing you know they will try to prevent citizens from owning any kind of handgun, then they will take away our hunting rifles, then our shotguns. Eventually, kids will be going to prison for having BB guns and water pistols! We can stop this lunacy by voting against the law banning assault rifles!"

QUESTIONABLE CLAIM

Questionable claim is the fallacy of using statements that are too broad or too exaggerated to be true. Words such as *all, every, never,* and *none* are often used in questionable claim statements. Examples could include, "*all* religious people are against abortion," "*every* pit bull is vicious," or "teachers *never* care about how students feel." As you can see, disproving a questionable claim fallacy requires only one exception.

"Between truth and the search for truth, I opt for the second." (Bernard Berenson)

PROVINCIALISM

Provincialism is the fallacy of looking at an issue or question only from your point of view, or the point of view of people like you. It is a fallacy of narrow-mindedness, of not seeing the viewpoints of others. For example, Maria, a wealthy person, argues against taxing the rich to provide social programs for the underprivileged. She doesn't care that these programs may help many people live better lives. All that matters to her are the effects of the programs on people like her. This fallacy is an easy trap to fall into, because the first tool that any of us have in interpreting the world around us is our own point of view. However, most people also use *empathy,* the skill of understanding the feelings and perspectives of others. The person using the provincialism fallacy either does not have the ability to use empathy or simply chooses not to.

"He who will not reason is a bigot; he who cannot is a fool; and he who dares not is a slave." (William Drummond)

FALSE APPEAL TO AUTHORITY

False appeal to authority is the fallacy of incorrectly relying on authority figures or experts to back up your argument. It is not always a fallacy to rely on authority figures to back up your point of view. After all, that is one purpose of research. But the authorities referred to should be real experts and have some special insight into the issue being discussed. The fallacy occurs when your expert is not really an authority in the area you are talking about, or when other experts seem to agree that your expert is wrong. For example, if you were trying to convince a friend that it is not always morally wrong to use animals in medical experiments, it would not seem appropriate to quote a famous movie star who happens to agree with your opinion. All by itself, having a famous name does not make anyone an authority. A more appropriate expert would be a doctor or a scientist.

FALSE APPEAL TO POPULARITY

False appeal to popularity is the fallacy of assuming that an idea is right because many people believe that it is. People using this fallacy believe that if an idea is popular it must be true. Do you know people who seem to base their own opinions on what others think? In an ethics class once, a student stated that she was in favor of the death penalty because she had read in the newspaper that 82% of Americans were for it. She asked, "How could that many people be wrong?" There are powerful arguments on both sides of the death penalty issue, but relying on popularity alone is not one of them. At different times in history the majority of humans have believed that the earth was flat; that it was the center of the universe; and that the stars were really small holes in the night sky, letting in light from the other side. No idea becomes true just because it is popular.

> "He who learns but does not think is lost! He who thinks but does not learn is in great danger."
> (Confucius)

CRITICAL THINKING

To improve your understanding of the "Dirty Dozen" fallacies, complete Critical Thinking Exercises 4A and 4B on pages 75-77.

■ Using Critical Thinking in Ethics

As stated earlier, *critical thinking* is primarily a problem-solving process. It requires open-minded, consistent, and creative reasoning. Critical thinking in ethics is more than an attitude or a state of mind. It is made up of several specific skills that almost anyone can learn. In fact, you have already practiced using these skills in this and earlier chapters. Now it is time to put these skills together to create a system for finding your own answers to ethical questions.

STEP I: CLEARLY STATE THE ETHICAL QUESTION UNDER CONSIDERATION

The first step in this critical thinking system is to state the ethical question as clearly and specifically as possible. Vague, general questions lead to vague, general answers. The question "Is lying right or wrong?" is too general to yield specific answers. Asking "Is it ever morally right to tell a lie?" is better, but the question can be narrowed down even further. Clear, specific questions about lying might include:

- Is it ever morally right to tell a lie to avoid hurting a close friend's feelings?

- Is it ever morally right to tell a lie to save another person's life?

- Is it ever morally right for a doctor to lie to dying patients about their odds of survival so that the patients will keep fighting for life?

Simply asking the right questions will not automatically give you the right answers. However, doing so can save a great deal of time and frustration later on. Once you have stated the question clearly and specifically, you are ready to start looking for answers.

STEP 2: RESEARCH TO FIND THE INFORMATION YOU NEED

An important assumption in critical thinking is that none of us know everything. We cannot find the best answers to many of our questions without looking outside of ourselves for additional information. Because information can be found in so many places, creativity is an especially important research tool. For example, assume that you were trying to answer this question: "Is it ever morally right for a doctor to lie to dying patients about their odds of survival so that the patients will keep fighting for life?" Following are only a few of the people and places where you might find helpful information and different points of view. Can you think of others?

- Library books and periodicals
- Your doctor and other medical professionals you may know
- Religious leaders
- People who have been diagnosed with serious illnesses

Once again, simply finding information will not, in itself, answer all of your questions. You may find yourself feeling overwhelmed by many widely different points of view. But once you gather your information and look closely at what you have found, you will be ready for the next step in the critical thinking process.

STEP 3: IDENTIFY POSSIBLE ANSWERS TO THE QUESTION

The next step is to identify the most logical alternative answers to your original ethical question. Try to narrow down your list of possible answers to the three or four alternatives that seem the strongest. To continue with the ethical question about whether doctors should tell their dying patients the truth about their conditions, these alternatives might include:

1. Doctors should always tell their dying patients the truth about the odds of their survival.

2. Doctors should never tell their dying patients the truth about the odds of their survival.

3. Doctors should only share this information with patients who have a mental attitude that would keep them from giving up.

4. Doctors should only share this information when patients are so close to dying that their attitude could not help them recover.

Notice that the alternatives chosen reflect more than just the "always" and "never" extremes. You might end up deciding that the best alternative in this case is either the "always" or the "never" answer. However, you will probably find many ethical questions for which the best answer is somewhere in between the extremes. Once you have identified these alternatives, you are ready for the next step.

> "Our life is what our thoughts make it." (Marcus Aurelius Antonius)

STEP 4: EVALUATE THE STRENGTHS AND WEAKNESSES OF EACH ALTERNATIVE

Your goal in Step 4 is to carefully consider the strong points and weak points of each alternative. One set of tools in this evaluation process are the *moral princi- ples* discussed in Chapter 2. (See Illustration 4-3.) They are the principles of ego- ism, utility, virtues, rights, and duties. (If you need a quick review of how to apply these principles, take a second look at Critical Thinking Exercise 2F on page 36.) The other set of tools are the *fallacies* presented earlier in this chapter. For example, it is considered a strength when one or more of the moral principles support an alternative. However, it would be considered a weakness if an alterna- tive violated a moral principle or contained any fallacies.

Illustration 4-3

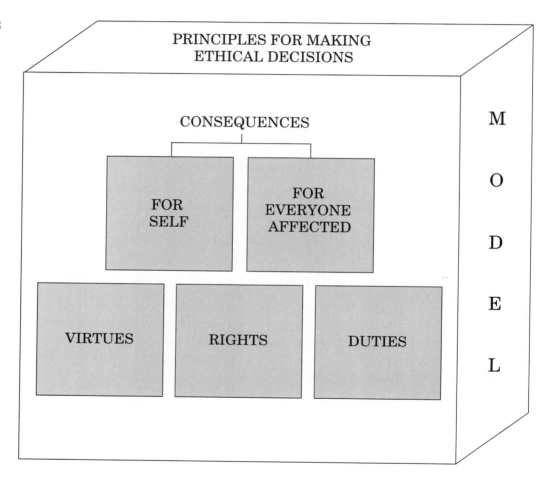

PRINCIPLES FOR MAKING ETHICAL DECISIONS

CONSEQUENCES

FOR SELF

FOR EVERYONE AFFECTED

VIRTUES

RIGHTS

DUTIES

MODEL

STEP 5: CHOOSE THE BEST ALTERNATIVE AND BE ABLE TO DEFEND IT

The final step in this critical thinking process is to decide which alternative repre- sents the best answer to your original ethical question. Obviously, you will need to consider the information you found in your research and the strengths and weak- nesses you noted in Step 4. The answer you choose will probably seem logical and right to you. Remember, however, that other people could look at the same ques- tion, go through the same steps, and choose different answers. They might find different information. Even if they found the same information, they might inter- pret and apply the principles and fallacies in different ways.

Being able to defend your answer does not mean that you are always able to convince others to agree with your opinion. Remember, the main goal of critical thinking is not to win all your arguments with others. It is more important that you be able to defend to yourself why you chose the answer you did, and that others be able to understand why you did so.

CRITICAL THINKING

To practice using the steps in critical thinking to find answers to actual ethical questions, complete Critical Thinking Exercise 4C on page 77-78.

1. The fallacies from the "Dirty Dozen" (Illustration 4-2 on page 65) that I notice myself using the most often are:

_____

_____

2. Several fallacies that I have heard other people use recently are:

_____

_____

3. Several people that I know who seem to be skilled at critical thinking are:

_____

_____

4. Journal.

a. The most important ideas that I learned in this chapter were:

_____

_____

b. Some of my strengths as a critical thinker are:

_____

_____

c. Some ways that I could use ideas from this chapter to become better at critical thinking are:

_____

_____

d. I would like to use the steps in critical thinking to find my "best answer" to this ethical question:

_____

_____

In the blank beside each statement, write the name of the fallacy that best describes it.

1. _____ "I think you are wrong about the danger of the sun's ultraviolet rays. After all, look how well our football team has been playing lately!"

2. _____ "I just can't support your idea about reserving the closest parking places for seniors. I don't care about the great things they've done for this school. I'm a sophomore, and I might have to park a half-mile away on rainy days."

3. _____ "Either you sell 100 candy bars in the fund-raiser or you don't really care about our band!"

4. _____ "If we don't let Luis be the yearbook editor he might tell his mother, the principal. Then she might accuse us of breaking a rule and suspend us. Then we might get behind in school and not graduate on time. Then we might not get accepted into college or technical school. We might never get a job! Let's just let him be the editor."

5. _____ "It is absolutely wrong for teenagers to use illegal drugs. People should protect their minds and bodies. Relying on drugs is no way to deal with your problems. It's just wrong! I do drink a lot of beer, though."

6. _____ "Last week I read that an elected city official was arrested for accepting a bribe. Today's paper said that another one was caught doing the same thing. So I have concluded that politicians are corrupt and dishonest."

7. _____ "I know for a fact that the square root of 16 is 8. I heard it directly from the sportscaster on Channel 8."

8. _____ "It is a tradition at this school that the 11th graders always go to lunch first. That's just the way it is, so that's how it should stay."

9. _____ "All blue-eyed people are intelligent."

10. _____ "Yes, I spray-painted one of the walls in the new gym. But Jerry painted a lot more than I did. He's the one who should be punished!"

11. _____ "This morning I had leftover pizza for breakfast. Then I wrecked the driver's education car. Evidently, pizza causes car wrecks."

12. _____ "A school survey showed that 90% of the students said that they would learn much better if school days lasted only two hours. Therefore, it must be true that we need shorter school days!"

Make up your own examples of each of the following fallacies:

1. Inconsistency

_____

_____

2. Two-Wrongs-Make-a-Right

_____

_____

3. Either/Or

_____

_____

4. Is/Ought

_____

_____

5. Red Herring

_____

_____

6. Hasty Generalization

_____

_____

7. Post Hoc

_____

_____

8. Slippery Slope

_____

_____

9. Questionable Claim

_____

_____

10. Provincialism

_____

_____

11. False Appeal to Authority

_____

_____

12. False Appeal to Popularity

_____

_____

Find your "best answer" to an ethical question by applying the steps in critical thinking that you have studied in this chapter. (Your teacher can help you choose an ethical question.)

Critical Thinking Exercise 4C, Page 71

Step 1: Clearly State the Ethical Question Under Consideration

Is it ever morally right to _____

_____ ?

Step 2: Research to Find the Information You Need

List possible sources of information here _____

_____

Step 3: Identify Possible Answers to the Question

A. _____

B. _____

C. _____

D. _____

Step 4: Evaluate the Strengths and Weaknesses of Each Alternative

Strengths   **Weaknesses**

A. _____   _____

B. _____   _____

C. _____   _____

D. _____   _____

Step 5: Choose the Best Alternative and Be Able to Defend It

Write your "best answer" and give the main reasons why you chose it over the other alternatives.

_____

_____

_____

_____

_____

_____

Reinforcement Exercises

1. Go on a "fallacy fishing trip" for a few days. Try to "catch" examples of people using some of the fallacies discussed in this chapter. Good "fallacy fishing holes" could include newspapers, television and radio talk shows, magazine articles about controversial issues, television news shows, and political debates. See who can come back with the most fallacies or the biggest "whoppers."

2. Write a one-page paper arguing either for or against some issue. Sounds boring, right? However, in this exercise your goal is to write the absolute *worst* arguments that you possibly can! The trick is to see how many fallacies you can squeeze into one page. Bonus points go to anyone who can get in all twelve!

3. Pick an ethical issue from one of the following chapters in this book. Then choose one ethical question related to that issue. Use the critical thinking system to find your best possible answer to that question.

4. In Your Own Words—Write your own definitions to the new terms and concepts you have learned in this chapter. Don't copy the words from the book, but paraphrase the definitions instead. What do they mean to you?

a. **Critical Thinking** — _____

_____

b. **Fallacies** — _____

_____

c. **Inconsistency** — _____

_____

d. **Two-Wrongs-Make-a-Right** — _____

_____

e. **Either/Or** — _____

_____

f. **Is/Ought** — _____

_____

g. **Red Herring** — _____

_____

h. **Hasty Generalization** — _____

_____

i. **Post Hoc** — _____

_____

j. **Slippery Slope** — _____

_____

k. **Questionable Claim** — _____

_____

l. **Provincialism** — _____

_____

m. False Appeal to Authority — _____

_____

n. False Appeal to Popularity — _____

_____

ETHICS IN THE WORKPLACE

OBJECTIVES

After completing this chapter, you will be able to:

■ 1. Define business ethics.

■ 2. Analyze assumptions about the relationship between ethics and success in business.

■ 3. Identify ethical issues common to the workplace environment.

■ 4. Apply critical thinking skills to analyze important ethical issues in the workplace.

■ Focus

Imagine that you have graduated from school and are ready to invest most of your money in starting a business. Your plan requires that you hire five employees to help get the company off the ground. You know that your success or failure will depend, as much as anything else, on the quality of work performed by these employees. First, list character traits that you would want to see in the people you hire. Then list character traits that you would consider unacceptable in new employees.

Preferred Employee Character Traits:

_____

_____

_____

_____

Unacceptable Employee Character Traits:

_____

_____

_____

_____

■ Ethics in Business

Many American high school students work in part-time jobs. Some even have full-time jobs during the summer and holiday breaks. Ethical issues, problems, and dilemmas exist in every type of business environment. But some people try to draw a distinction between the ethics of private life and the ethics of the workplace. (See Illustration 5-1). Is business ethics somehow different from personal ethics? In this chapter you will investigate this question and learn how to apply your critical thinking skills to ethical issues in the workplace.

Illustration 5-1

■ What Is Business Ethics?

Business ethics is the branch of ethics in which people attempt to apply moral principles to workplace questions. These principles are the same ones that people use when making ethical decisions at home and in school. You studied many of these principles in Chapter 2. However, the workplace also presents some unique types of ethical problems. This fact has led some people to make questionable assumptions about the relationship between succeeding in business and acting ethically.

ASSUMPTIONS ABOUT ETHICS AND SUCCESS IN BUSINESS

Gandhi's Seven Sins:
- **Wealth without work**
- **Pleasure without conscience**
- **Knowledge without character**
- **Commerce without morality**
- **Science without humility**
- **Worship without sacrifice**
- **Politics without principle.**

An *assumption* is a belief, stated as a fact, that cannot be proven true or false. If valid, these assumptions would make a rational discussion of ethics in business more difficult. Read critically through the assumptions and explanations below, looking for logical strengths and weaknesses.

Success in business can only be measured in terms of money. Each year, *Fortune* magazine publishes a special issue on the "Fortune 500," a listing of the most successful corporations in America. In reality, the list represents the 500 American corporations that made the most money in the previous year. It is often assumed that profit is the only factor in measuring success or failure in the world of business. But is money really all there is to "success" for a company? Are there any other factors that should be considered?

Ethics are important in life, but irrelevant in business. This assumption is based on the belief that a "good person" may be one who acts morally, but a "good business" is one that makes a lot of money. If the only goal of a business is to make money, why confuse things by throwing in the idea of ethics? Just as the decision to wear blue pants instead of brown pants is not an ethical issue, neither is the decision of how a business chooses to make money.

All's fair in love, war, and business. If money is the only measure of success, and if how people make money does not matter, then there are no limits to what can be done. If you can make more money through false advertising, deceiving customers, or treating your employees unfairly, then those types of actions become acceptable. As long as you make a large profit, no one else has the right to question the morality of how you did it.

Acting ethically in business means you will always make less money. This assumption implies that, while people should normally try to live by high ethical standards, to do so in the workplace involves too much financial sacrifice. It is the belief that being dishonest is always more profitable than being honest.

Acting ethically in business means you will always make more money. At the other end of the spectrum is the assumption that ethical behavior always leads to financial success. This idea is based on the simple notion that the good guys always win and the bad guys always lose. Even if this were true, the logical next step would be to decide to act ethically because you wanted to make more money. Is that really how ethics works?

CRITICAL THINKING

How would you respond to each of the preceding assumptions about the relationship between acting ethically and being successful in the business world? Complete Critical Thinking Exercise 5A on page 91.

THE CURRENT STATUS OF BUSINESS ETHICS IN AMERICA

Ethics is a growing concern in today's workplace. Executives and managers in corporations all across the country are emphasizing the need for their workers to be ethical people. More than 85% of the largest corporations in America currently have written codes of ethics for their employees to follow. A **code of ethics** is a written set of ethical guidelines that workers are expected to follow. Many companies are also investing in resources such as ethics training programs and ethics advice hot lines to give employees guidance when facing ethical decisions in their jobs. Why are these businesses going to this much trouble over ethics?

Many businesses have found that unethical actions by employees can be expensive. American companies lose billions of dollars in profits each year due to actions such as employee theft, abuse of sick time, and drug and alcohol abuse in the workplace. In addition, corporations are often held legally responsible for the actions of their employees. This means that companies can be sued when their employees act in unethical and illegal ways. Businesses usually act in ways that they believe will lead to higher profits. Evidently, many businesses are becoming convinced that investing in employee ethics will pay off in the long run by increasing profits.

When explaining why they choose to act ethically at work, however, most employees mention more than ethics training, hot lines, and company codes of ethics. More often, workers find a personal motivation for acting ethically. Recently, about 100 community college students were asked to complete an anonymous survey. On average, these students were 29 years of age, with more than 10 years of experience in the workplace. They were asked whether being an ethical person in the workplace was important to them, and why or why not.

Answering yes, 93 percent of the students said that being an ethical person in the workplace was important to them. When asked to explain why, the students mentioned the following reasons. Which ones seem to reflect the way you might have answered the question?

Top 10 Reasons for Being Ethical in the Workplace

#10. I want my family and friends to be proud of my actions, not ashamed of them.

#9. Ethics is more important than money. It's best to earn money honestly.

#8. Acting ethically helps me avoid negative consequences such as ugly fights over power and money, expensive lawsuits, and unsafe products that could harm other people.

#7. Ethical people tend to attract other ethical people, and I want to work with ethical customers and co-workers.

#6. I believe in treating others the way I want to be treated, and I want to be treated ethically.

#5. Acting ethically helps me earn the respect of others. It shows that I have respect for myself and others.

#4. I want to do my part to make the world a better place, to be a role model for others. I don't want to just "go with the flow" and conform to unethical standards around me.

#3. Acting ethically makes me feel like I'm a good person. It is helping me become the kind of person that I want to be.

#2. Ethical behavior is good for business. It gains the trust of customers, so they keep coming back. It also helps my company become more orderly and efficient.

#1. The workplace is not separate from the rest of my life. I believe that people who act unethically in business act the same way in the rest of their lives. I want to be consistently ethical in all aspects of my life.

■ Important Ethical Issues in Business

Even for people who commit themselves to acting ethically and responsibly, the workplace presents many challenging moral issues and problems. There is not enough space in this chapter to discuss them all, but here are a few of the most basic and common ethical issues with which employees are faced.

EMPLOYEE DUTIES

You learned in Chapter 2 that a *moral duty* is an ethical obligation that one individual has to others. Therefore, **employee duties** are the ethical obligations that employees have to their employers. Employees that fulfill these duties are often rewarded with promotions and raises. On the other hand, employees who do not fulfill their obligations may be disciplined, demoted, or fired.

Commonly accepted employee duties include honesty, loyalty to the company, and giving a fair day's work. However, these duties are not always so clear-cut. Sometimes an employer's expectations can be unrealistic and even unethical. What if a business believes its employees have a duty to place a higher priority on the company than on their families? What if employees know that a product is unsafe, but are told to keep quiet about it based on their duty to remain loyal to the company?

> "The foundation of morality is to have done, once and for all, with lying."
> (T. H. Huxley)

CRITICAL THINKING

To further explore the ethical issue of employee duties, complete Critical Thinking Exercise 5B on page 92.

EMPLOYEE RIGHTS

As you learned in Chapter 2, *rights* refer to how an individual is entitled to be treated by others. **Employee rights**, therefore, are those things that workers are owed by their employers. Earlier in American history, it was assumed that employees had few, if any, such rights. Men, women, and even children worked long hours for very little money, often in dangerous surroundings. Employees who got sick or injured, as well as those who complained about unfair treatment, were simply fired and replaced. These types of abuses helped lead to the establishment of trade unions. Powerless employees banded together into powerful groups. Most businesses could not afford to replace all of their workers at once and were forced to give in to employee demands for basic human rights in the workplace.

Today, a list of commonly accepted employee rights would include safe working conditions, equal opportunity in hiring and promotions, and fair pay. As with the issue of employee duties, however, there are areas of disagreement over employee rights. For example, consider the difference between employee rights and employee benefits. *Benefits* are features that companies may not be ethically required to provide for their workers, but offer anyway to attract high-quality employees. Having two weeks of paid vacation or paid sick leave per year might be seen by some employees as a *right*, but viewed by company management as a *benefit*.

> "Every young man would do well to remember that all successful business stands on the foundation of morality."
> (Henry Ward Beecher)

CRITICAL THINKING

To see how well you understand the concept of employee rights, complete Critical Thinking Exercise 5C on page 92.

CONFLICT OF INTEREST

A **conflict of interest** occurs when people who have agreed to act in the best interests of others choose to act in their own interests instead. (See Illustration 5-2.) In business, "others" refers to the company or organization for whom an employee works. Businesses in America rank conflicts of interest among the most common and troubling ethical problems their employees face today. The results of these conflicts can include poor decisions made on behalf of the business and the loss of trust between employer and employee.

Illustration 5-2

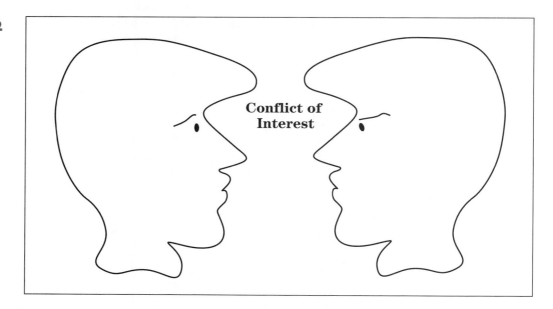

The following case study offers an example of a situation containing a potential conflict of interest. As you read it, keep in mind the Critical Thinking model from Chapter 4.

■ CASE STUDY Conflict of Interest

Taylor oversees the purchasing of office supplies for the Smells-Good Socks Corporation. His job is to buy quality supplies for the company at low prices, helping Smells-Good to make a higher total profit. Today, Taylor got a personal letter from the DimView Lighting Company. The letter stated that if he purchased a large order of bulbs from DimView, they would treat Taylor's family to a free vacation at a beautiful Florida beach resort. Taylor knows that DimView's light bulbs cost a little more and do not last quite as long as the brand he normally purchases, but the vacation offer is very tempting. "Besides," he says to himself, "no one really pays attention to what brand of bulb we use. I work hard and I deserve this trip. It's not like I'm hurting anyone, is it?"

CRITICAL THINKING

Analyze Taylor's ethical dilemma by answering the questions in Critical Thinking Exercise 5D on page 93.

WHISTLE-BLOWING

Occasionally, workers find out that the businesses they work for are acting unethically and even illegally. These workers then face the difficult decision of whether or not to blow the whistle. **Whistle-blowing** is the act of reporting unethical or illegal actions by one's superiors or peers to authorities or to the media. (See Illustration 5-3.) Blowing the whistle on one's own company requires a great deal of courage. Whistle-blowers are sometimes viewed as traitors by their employers and co-workers. They are often punished or fired.

Illustration 5-3

Whistle-blowing cases can be difficult to resolve. The businesses often deny the charges made by whistle-blowers. The public is left unsure of whom to believe. After all, not all charges made by whistle-blowers are true. There are cases in which angry employees make up false allegations to embarrass their companies. And sometimes whistle-blowers simply get the facts wrong and make inaccurate assumptions. However, there are many cases in which the whistle-blowers' charges are proven to be correct. Their actions can result in businesses having to change their policies, admitting that their actions have been unethical or illegal.

Whistle-blowers have saved lives by revealing dangerous products. They have saved taxpayers billions of dollars by speaking out against corrupt practices between businesses and government agencies. They have brought wrongdoers to justice by courageously testifying against their own companies in courtrooms. Are those results worth risking one's job for? Many whistle-blowers seem to think so.

The following is a case study highlighting the issue of whistle-blowing. Again, keep the Critical Thinking model in mind as you consider Connie's dilemma.

"The great power and privilege I had forgone of earning money by my own labor occurred to me." (Frances Anne Kimble)

■ CASE STUDY Whistle-blowing

Connie is a new quality control inspector for the Veri-Safe Toy Company, makers of "CutiePie Dolls." The best-selling dolls in the toy market, the CutiePie dolls use teeth and moveable jaws to eat tiny toy fruit pies that are sold separately. One day, while picking up a handful of these dolls, Connie gashed her finger on one of the teeth. Connie's supervisor gave her a bandage and told her not to report the accident to anyone. When Connie asked why, the supervisor said that Veri-Safe was being sued because several children had been cut by the doll teeth. The company's leaders were officially denying that the teeth were dangerous. However, the leaders had ordered that all reports of such injuries in the factory be destroyed. Also, all employees were to be reminded of the importance of loyalty and secrecy at times like this. Connie asked why the company didn't just make the dolls safer. The supervisor replied that the dolls couldn't eat the pies unless the teeth were sharp. As Connie walked back to her work area she noticed the new company product she was wearing. Her bandage was covered with pictures of CutiePie Dolls.

"Ninety percent of success is just showing up." (Woody Allen)

CRITICAL THINKING

Should Connie blow the whistle on Veri-Safe? Analyze Connie's ethical dilemma in Critical Thinking Exercise 5E on page 94.

■ Conclusion

No matter what your career goals are, you will find ethical issues, questions, and problems in your future profession. You will need to rely on your ethical principles and your critical thinking skills to make difficult decisions. Ethics in the workplace may not be all that different from ethics in private life. Maybe there is just more money at stake.

I. **Is being an ethical person in the workplace important to you? Why or why not?**

_____

_____

2. **Do you think being ethical in business is different somehow from being ethical in other areas of life? Why or why not?**

_____

_____

3. **If you have had a job before, write down one ethical issue, question, or problem that you had to deal with in that job.**

_____

_____

4. **As you look back now on that issue, question, or problem, how do you feel about the way you made your decision? How do you feel about what you decided to do? Would you do anything different today?**

_____

_____

_____

_____

5. Journal.

a. The most important ideas that I learned in this chapter were:

_____

_____

b. To me, being "successful" in the workplace means:

_____

_____

c. I believe that my strengths as an ethical employee are:

_____

_____

d. One area in which I could become a more ethical employee is:

_____

_____

Read each of the following assumptions about the relationship between ethics and business. Circle either the word agree or the word disagree beside each assumption, then explain why you agree or disagree.

1. Success in business can only be measured in terms of money.

AGREE   DISAGREE

_____

_____

2. Ethics are important in life, but irrelevant in business.

AGREE   DISAGREE

_____

_____

3. All's fair in love, war, and business.

AGREE   DISAGREE

_____

_____

4. Acting ethically in business means you will always make less money.

AGREE   DISAGREE

_____

_____

5. Acting ethically in business means you will always make more money.

AGREE   DISAGREE

_____

_____

1. List ethical duties to their employers that you believe all employees should fulfill.

_____

_____

_____

_____

2. List unfair or unethical expectations of their employees that some businesses might have.

_____

_____

_____

_____

1. List moral rights that you believe all employees are entitled to be given by their employers.

_____

_____

_____

2. List benefits that employees sometimes think of as basic rights.

_____

_____

_____

_____

1. **Would it be a conflict of interest if Taylor ordered the DimView light bulbs and accepted the trip to Florida? Explain why or why not.**

_____

_____

2. **What if DimView's light bulbs were actually of higher quality and less expensive than the brand normally ordered? Would it still be a conflict of interest for Taylor to order the DimView bulbs and accept the trip to Florida? Would it be wrong for him to accept the trip?**

_____

_____

3. **Apply the critical thinking model you learned in Chapter 4 to find your best solution to the case study about Taylor and conflict of interest.**

Step 1: Clearly state the ethical question under consideration.

_____

_____

Step 2: Research to find the information you need. (What sources of information could help Taylor decide what he should do?)

_____

_____

Step 3: Identify possible answers to the question.

_____

_____

Step 4: Evaluate the strengths and weaknesses of each alternative.

<u>Strengths</u>	<u>Weaknesses</u>
_____	_____
_____	_____

Step 5: Choose the best alternative and be able to defend it.

_____

_____

Critical Thinking Exercise 5E, Page 88

Apply the critical thinking model you learned in Chapter 4. Find your best solution to Connie's ethical dilemma.

Step 1: Clearly state the ethical question under consideration.

_____

_____

Step 2: Research to find the information you need. (What sources of information could help Connie decide what she should do?)

_____

_____

Step 3: Identify possible answers to the question.

_____

_____

Step 4: Evaluate the strengths and weaknesses of each alternative.

Strengths   **Weaknesses**

_____   _____

_____   _____

Step 5: Choose the best alternative and be able to defend it.

_____

_____

1. Survey people who have experience in business, asking them for their opinions about ethics in business. Make your own list of questions based on ideas presented in this chapter.

2. Create your own hypothetical corporation. Decide what kind of business you want it to be and give it a fun name. Then write a code of ethics for your company. Your code of ethics should include (a) a few basic ethical rules that your employees will be expected to follow, (b) a list of employee duties, and (c) a list of employee rights. Also, indicate what kinds of resources you would make available to help your employees make ethical decisions.

3. Write a biographical paper or a book report about a successful leader in American business or industry. Were this person's ethical standards important to his or her success? What kinds of ethical principles did the person recommend to other businesspeople?

4. Pick one occupation that you are interested in learning more about. Then research some of the ethical issues that people in that occupation have to deal with. Your research sources could include library books and periodicals and even interviews with people already working in that job.

5. List the ethical obligations or responsibilities that corporations should have to each of the following groups. In other words, what does a business *owe* each group?

   a. Its employees _____

   _____

   b. Its customers/consumers _____

   _____

   c. The community/society to which it belongs _____

   _____

   d. Its stockholders_____

   _____

   e. Its competitors _____

   _____

6. Paraphrase the following key terms from this chapter.

6. Paraphrase the following key terms from this chapter. What do they mean to you?

a. **Business ethics** _____

_____

b. **Code of ethics** _____

_____

c. **Employee duties** _____

_____

d. **Employee rights** _____

_____

e. **Conflict of interest** _____

_____

f. **Whistle-blowing** _____

_____

ETHICS IN GOVERNMENT AND CITIZENSHIP

OBJECTIVES

After completing this chapter, you will be able to:

■ 1. Define government ethics.

■ 2. Identify common ethical issues in public service.

■ 3. Identify safeguards that promote ethical actions by government officials.

■ 4. Describe ethical responsibilities of citizens.

■ 5. Apply moral principles to specific ethical issues in government and citizenship.

■ Focus

Toshi is a sophomore at a local community college. She also has a part-time job as an aide in the mayor's office. Yesterday, a large box with a red ribbon tied around it was delivered to the office. Inside the box were dozens of expensive watches, gifts to the mayor's staff from the Tik-Tok Watch Corporation. Toshi knew that, for the past few weeks, the city government had been debating a change in the local zoning laws. Changing the laws would allow Tik-Tok to save over a million dollars in purchasing land for a new watch factory. Local officials, business leaders, and citizens were bitterly divided over the issue. No one was sure how the final city council vote would turn out.

Toshi saw a card attached to the red ribbon. The card read, "Dear friends at City Hall: We at Tik-Tok are excited that we may soon have our new factory in your community. We appreciate whatever help you can give us in getting the zoning laws changed. Please keep the watches as a token of our goodwill and friendship." As Toshi put the card down, she heard one of the other staffers calling her, "Hey, Toshi, do you want a gold watch, a silver one, or both?"

WHAT DO YOU THINK?

The following questions ask your views about some of the ethical issues in Toshi's case. Write down your honest opinions. You have the right to keep your moral beliefs private. You are free to share them with your teacher and your classmates if you choose, but it is your choice. No one will force you to.

1. Do you think the free watches are really just for "goodwill and friendship?" If not, what other reasons might Tik-Tok have for giving the watches away?

_____

_____

_____

_____

2. How do you think the town's citizens would feel if they found out that the mayor's staff had accepted the Tik-Tok gifts under these circumstances?

_____

_____

_____

_____

3. Suppose the city council had already voted to change the zoning laws and the watches were Tik-Tok's way of thanking the mayor's staff for their help and support? Would that make a difference in your decision about whether the watches should be accepted? Why?

_____

_____

_____

_____

"If men were angels, no government would be necessary." (James Madison)

Government officials and employees are often referred to as "public servants." Though some people separate elected officials from career civil employees, they will be considered together in this study. Both groups are supposed to act in the best interests of the people they represent or serve. These public employees face many of the same ethical issues and problems that employees face in other professions and careers. However, because public servants work *for the people* rather than for a corporation, they also face some unique ethical issues. **Government ethics** is the branch of ethics in which people attempt to apply moral principles to the ethical questions arising in public service. In this chapter you will investigate some of those questions. You will discover tools that our society relies on to promote ethical actions by government officials and employees. You will also learn about the important role that citizens must play in maintaining an ethical system of government.

■ Government Ethics in American History

In many ways, the United States of America began as an experiment. No country quite like it had ever existed before. Most of the established nations of the mid-1700s were *monarchies*, meaning they were under the control of one sovereign ruler, such as a king or queen. But the founders of the United States believed that monarchies were morally wrong. This judgment was based on the moral principle that all individuals have equal rights. The American founders believed that the principle of individual rights was the only possible foundation for a moral system of government. After all, if all people have equal rights, then poor and weak citizens in a nation should have the same voice in social decisions as the rich and powerful. Therefore, the founders held that *democracy,* or government by the people, was the only moral form of government. Some of these beliefs are seen clearly in the following excerpt from the Declaration of Independence.

> We hold these truths to be self-evident, that all men are created equal, that they are endowed by their Creator with certain unalienable Rights, that among these are Life, Liberty, and the pursuit of Happiness. That to secure these rights governments are instituted among Men, deriving their just powers from the consent of the governed. That whenever any Form of Government becomes destructive of these ends, it is the Right of the People to alter or to abolish it, and to institute new Government, laying its foundation on such principles and organizing its powers in such form, as to them shall seem most likely to effect their Safety and Happiness.

"To suppose that any form of government will secure liberty or happiness without any virtue in the people is a chimerical [unrealistic] idea. If there is sufficient virtue and intelligence in the community, it will be exercised in the selection of these men. So that we do not depend on their virtue, but in the people who are to choose them." (James Madison)

CRITICAL THINKING

Have you ever thought about the fact that the Declaration of Independence is a statement of moral principles? To better understand its meaning, complete Critical Thinking Exercise 6A on page 109.

CHECKS AND BALANCES IN GOVERNMENT

The founders of the United States were motivated by a desire for liberty. However, they also understood several practical realities about how governments operate in the real world. One of those realities is that people with power often attempt to get more power. Therefore, the founders set up a three-branch system of *checks and balances*, limiting the amount of power that one person or group could obtain. The *legislative* branch, consisting of the House of Representatives and the Senate, writes the laws. The *executive* branch, or the presidential administration, ensures that the laws are carried out, and has limited power to veto laws written by the legislative branch. The *judicial* branch, or the courts, interpret the laws and determine whether they are consistent with the Constitution. This system produces a *balance of power* in which each branch is limited by the power of the others.

As stated previously, the founders believed that moral governments must be built on individual rights and liberties. However, a second reality the founders understood about government was that individual rights can sometimes conflict with the *common good,* or what is best for the group as a whole. Which is more important, the rights of individuals or the overall welfare of society? This question is one of the great challenges of democracies. In the Constitution, the founders set up a system designed to protect both. The executive and legislative branches have an obvious interest in promoting the welfare of the group, because keeping a majority of "the group" happy is essential for reelection. However, certain individual rights are guaranteed in the Constitution. It is the responsibility of the courts to ensure that laws do not infringe on those individual rights. Again you can see that the branches of government both complement and limit each other.

CRITICAL THINKING

To analyze the implications of the practical realities of government, answer the questions in Critical Thinking Exercise 6B on page 109.

Ethical Issues in Government

Over its first 200 or so years, the new American government system was tested by many difficult ethical issues, questions, and scandals. Terms such as *Watergate* and *Iran-Contra Arms Scandal* have entered our everyday language to refer to such scandals. However, there have also been many earlier government ethics scandals at the federal, state, and local levels. Each of these scandals had its own unique qualities, but at least two issues have presented almost constant problems in maintaining government ethics.

CONFLICT OF INTEREST

You learned in Chapter 5 that *conflicts of interest* occur when people who have agreed to act in the best interests of others choose to act in their own best interests instead. (See Illustration 6-1.) People in public service have agreed to act in the best interests of the citizens that they represent. These citizens are the *employers* of the government officials, whose salaries are paid by the citizens' tax dollars. In return for their salaries, public servants agree, often by taking an oath, to act in the best interests of their constituents.

Government officials can be guilty of conflicts of interest in many ways. A government employee could sell national secrets to a foreign government. A political candidate might accept campaign contributions or personal bribes in exchange for future political favors. A government office worker could accept bribes in exchange for purchasing products from certain companies. When officials are guilty of conflicts of interest, the citizens they represent often feel betrayed. Take another look at Toshi's case study at the beginning of this chapter. Can you find the apparent conflict of interest involved?

Illustration 6-1

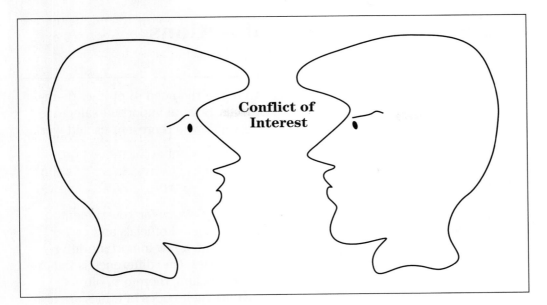

Conflict of Interest

THE CORRUPTING POWER OF MONEY

Money and politics have been closely bound together throughout world history. The influence of television has worked to make those bonds stronger than ever. Candidates, especially at the state and national levels, have learned that "air time" on television is essential to getting elected. However, buying that air time is expensive. One recent estimate found that, to adequately finance their reelection campaigns, U. S. senators must raise more than $20,000 per week during their six-year terms in office! This never-ending need for money creates temptations for ethical abuses such as bribery and conflict of interest.

As the saying goes, "There ain't no such thing as a free lunch." It's fairly safe to assume that when people give you money or other things of value, they expect something in return. Political contributors who donate large amounts of money often expect influence over the politicians they support. The contributors want their points of view to be listened to a little more closely than everyone else's. Is that unethical? The courts have held that this system is legal and constitutional. However, many people, including some politicians, are concerned that the influence of money is undermining our democratic process. A congressional representative from Massachusetts stated, "To be an ethical politician today means to be an ingrate. I have to be able to take $10,000 from relative strangers and then act like that money has no effect on my actions." Some have even said that the golden rule of politics is, "Those with the gold make the rules." Do you think this is how the founders meant for our government to operate? Is this system consistent with the meaning of democracy?

CRITICAL THINKING

Analyze ethical issues in government more closely by answering the questions in Critical Thinking Exercise 6C on page 110.

"By all means let us consider how to assist in the establishment of higher moral standards in the official conduct of the government, but at the same time let us realize that we cannot hope to assist the government in this regard unless we are willing to assist ourselves and each other in the establishment of higher moral standards as between man and man in private life." (Harold Ickes)

Safeguards That Promote Ethical Actions in Government

Over the years, American citizens have grown to see the need to protect themselves from ethical abuses by government officials. Several important safeguards have evolved to help ensure that the public servants who represent us and work for us act ethically and legally.

CODES OF ETHICS

Similar to those for workers in corporations, *codes of ethics* for government employees are written ethical guidelines that both elected officials and career employees are expected to follow. There are, however, a few important differences between government codes and corporate codes. One difference is that government codes of ethics are written by legislators and, therefore, often become laws as well. Government officials violating their codes of ethics are also breaking the law and can be punished more harshly. A second difference has to do with enforcement of the codes. Business codes of ethics are enforced by employers, who use the codes to control their employees. Government codes, on the other hand, are enforced at a *peer* level. A senator suspected of violating a rule in the Senate code of ethics is often investigated and disciplined by other senators. Can you see some advantages and disadvantages of such a system?

THE NEWS MEDIA

A second safeguard that Americans rely on to maintain ethics in government is the news media. Throughout American history, reporters, editors, and political cartoonists have often led the battle against corruption in government. The Watergate conspiracy of the 1970s, which led to the only resignation of an American president, was one of many such ethical scandals uncovered by reporters. Since its creation, the television news media has taken on the same responsibility, focusing public attention on unethical and illegal activities by officials.

Historically, governments have tried to limit the power of the press. In many of the European monarchies described earlier, the press was controlled by government officials. News stories that reflected badly on the government were forbidden. The founders of America understood that the press has an important role in protecting our democracy from unethical political leaders. Thus, freedom of the press was among the first rights spelled out in the Bill of Rights.

> Amendment 1: "Congress shall make no law respecting an establishment of religion, or prohibiting the free exercise thereof; or abridging the freedom of speech, *or of the press;* or the right of the people peaceably to assemble, and to petition the government for a redress of grievances." [italics added]

This guarantee of a free press does not answer all of the questions about how the press should treat government officials. Sometimes reporters act in ways that raise ethical questions, too. Former Secretary of State Henry Kissinger once had his household garbage stolen by a reporter who was looking to find evidence that would embarrass Kissinger. Candidate Gary Hart was forced to withdraw from a presidential election after reporters, hidden in the bushes outside his home, wrote that a young model spent the night in the house when Hart's wife was out of town. Candidate, and later President, Bill Clinton protested that the media seemed more interested in allegations about his private life than in the policies and programs he believed in. Government officials sometimes complain of being intimidated and harassed by reporters who watch their every move. For all of their problems, however, the free press and news media serve as powerful tools to protect American citizens from ethical abuses by those in government.

INFORMED AND INVOLVED CITIZENS

The most important safeguard to prevent unethical actions in American government are the citizens themselves. Codes of ethics are just words on paper unless citizens demand that the codes be enforced. If people aren't listening or don't care enough to get involved, news stories just fill time or space between advertisements. In the following section, you will learn more about the most important part of government ethics, the responsibilities of citizens.

CRITICAL THINKING

To reflect on the strengths and weaknesses of the ethical safeguards, complete Critical Thinking Exercise 6D on page 111.

■ The Responsibilities of Citizen-Leaders

In the old monarchies, the responsibilities of the citizens was to serve and obey the monarch. But democracy is government "by the people." Our American founders meant for the government to serve and obey the will of the people. The citizens are not just to be followers, but **citizen-leaders**, meaning individuals who are actively involved in the process of government. In democratic governments, citizens lead their leaders. This was part of Abraham Lincoln's message in the Gettysburg Address when he described a government "of the people, by the people, and for the people." What are the responsibilities of these citizen-leaders in a democracy?

STAY INFORMED

What would you think if you found out that the president didn't read newspapers or watch television news? Could the president not be very interested in national or world events and still be an effective leader? Of course not. Leaders have an obligation to keep themselves informed. Citizen-leaders have the same obligation. More sources of information are available to citizens today than at any other time in history. Early in our nation's history, it sometimes took weeks for voters in some parts of the United States to find out who won a presidential election or whether a law was passed. Today, citizens in Hawaii, Alaska, Puerto Rico, or Guam can sit at home, watching live as leg-

"If a nation expects to be ignorant and free in a state of civilization, it expects what never was and will never be.... If we are to guard against ignorance and remain free it is the responsibility of every American to be informed." (Thomas Jefferson)

islators debate and vote on a bill. Staying informed about local, national, and world events is not difficult, but it is important.

BE CRITICAL THINKERS

Simply being aware of events around you is not enough. Citizen-leaders also have the responsibility to develop their abilities to understand what these events mean. This is where critical thinking fits in. Government "by the people" requires that the people use wisdom. This does not mean that you have to carry a step-by-step guide to critical thinking with you wherever you go. Critical thinking for citizen-leaders means asking tough questions, watching for fallacies in what people say, and measuring the actions of government officials against ethical principles.

VOTE

In 1990, the people of Poland elected labor leader Lech Walesa as president in their first free election in more than a generation. One report stated that more than 95 percent of the eligible citizens of Poland voted. Several Polish citizens told reporters that they had often envied the fact that people in free countries such as the United States could vote so easily. In contrast, when George Bush was elected as America's president in 1988, barely 50 percent of the American citizens who were eligible to vote did so. And only 55 percent of adult Americans voted in the 1992 presidential election won by Bill Clinton.

Americans are often quick to list voting among their civic duties. Ironically, many Americans do not bother to vote, even in important national elections. It is not uncommon in smaller, local elections to see turnouts of fewer than one-third of eligible voters. Why is participation so low? Many people do not seem to believe that their vote will make a difference. Others are just too busy to register or to vote. Some may not be informed enough to know what the election is about or where to vote. In contrast, in the past few decades, people all over the globe have bravely stood up to tyrannical governments. They have been willing to sacrifice their lives so that their children and grandchildren could have the freedom to live and vote in democracies. If government by the people is really for the common good, then a basic responsibility of a citizen-leader is to be a voter.

DEMAND ETHICAL ACTIONS BY GOVERNMENT OFFICIALS

What is a "good" mayor, governor, representative, senator, or president? Is it one who agrees with you on controversial issues? Is it one who spends lots of government money on projects in your community? Americans sometimes expect little more from their leaders, and politicians have sometimes lived down to these short-term expectations. But another responsibility of citizen-leaders is that they hold their representatives to higher ethical standards. One positive side-effect of the government scandals of the past two decades is that American citizens and leaders have seen the need to raise those ethical standards. Government codes of ethics have been written and strengthened. The news media has helped by conducting its own investigations of corruption. Some officials whose actions did not measure up to these higher standards have seen their political careers end in disgrace. It is unrealistic for citizen-leaders to expect that their representatives agree with them on every issue. It is very realistic to demand that the actions of those representatives should be consistent with ethical ideals such as honesty, integrity, and honor.

GET INVOLVED

The next step in citizen-leader responsibility is involvement in the political process. This does not mean that everyone must run for elected office. It does mean that citizens need to make their opinions and wishes known. This can be done by participation in political parties, by writing or calling officials to tell them what you think about issues, or by participating in other special-interest political groups. In recent years, such citizen involvement has led to new laws protecting animals and the environment, to stricter ethical rules for political officials, and to more fair treatment for many people in our society. On the other hand, a government that is supposed to obey the will of the people cannot do that if the people don't make clear what their will is.

BE ETHICAL THEMSELVES

In some ways, governments are like social mirrors. Citizens looking at their governments often see the best and the worst of themselves. For example, many social experts describe *materialism,* an excessive concern for possessions and wealth, as a common problem in America today. So it shouldn't be too surprising that the corrupting influence of money is a serious ethical problem in our government. Political leaders are people, too, and they often reflect the values of their societies. For this reason, the founders of the United States were as concerned about the ethical character of future American citizens as they were about the ethics of their leaders.

It has been said that most people get the kind of government that they deserve. If this is true, then one of the best ways to improve the ethical climate of the American government is to improve the ethical character of the American people. And that starts with you.

CRITICAL THINKING

Critical Thinking Exercise 6E on pages 111 and 112 gives you an opportunity to agree or disagree with some of the ideas in this section. What do you think?

"There is no form of government but what may be a blessing to the people if well administered.... This government is likely to be administered for a course of years, and can only end in despotism as other forms have done before it, when the people shall become so corrupt as to need a despot government, being incapable of any other." (Benjamin Franklin)

1. Consider each of the following responsibilities of citizen-leaders. Explain what actions you could take in each area to become a more mature citizen and improve the ethical climate of your nation, community, or school.

Stay Informed

_____

_____

_____

Be a Critical Thinker

_____

_____

_____

Vote

_____

_____

_____

Demand Ethical Actions by Elected Officials

_____

_____

_____

Get Involved

_____

_____

_____

Be Ethical Yourself

_____

_____

_____

2. Journal.

    a. The most important ideas that I learned in this chapter were:

_____

_____

_____

    b. Some of my strengths as a citizen are:

_____

_____

_____

    c. One ethical issue or problem in government that concerns me right now is:

_____

_____

_____

Analyze the excerpt from the Declaration of Independence and answer the following questions:

Critical Thinking Exercise 6A, Page 99

I. What rights did the founders believe all humans are entitled to?

_____

_____

2. Why do we have governments? What is their purpose?

_____

_____

3. How should citizens react when a government is not fulfilling its purpose?

_____

_____

Answer these questions about the conflicts caused by the practical realities of government.

Critical Thinking Exercise 6B, Page 100

I. The *balance of powers* in federal and state governments leads to many conflicts among the different branches. These conflicts are reported on television news and in newspapers almost every day. Give an example of a recent controversy or issue in which two or more branches of government have clashed or disagreed. Which branch ended up getting its way? Why?

_____

_____

2. The government's dual responsibilities to protect individual rights and to promote the welfare of the larger group have also often clashed. Using the news media again, find and describe a recent issue in which you see such a conflict. Did the principle of rights or the principle of utility end up being chosen as the top priority? Why?

_____

_____

_____

1. **Locate a news story about a possible conflict of interest involving a government official or employee. Then analyze the story by answering the following questions.**

   a. **Briefly describe the facts of the situation.**

   _____

   _____

   _____

   b. **What were the consequences to the people involved?**

   _____

   _____

   _____

   c. **Which ethical principles were (or might have been) violated?**

   _____

   _____

   _____

2. **List several changes that America could make in its political system that would lessen the corrupting influence of money.**

   _____

   _____

   _____

1. As mentioned in the text, government codes of ethics are written, interpreted, and often enforced by the same legislators who are supposed to follow them. List some strengths and weaknesses that you see in this type of system.

Critical Thinking Exercise 6D, Page 103

Strengths

_____

_____

_____

Weaknesses

_____

_____

_____

2. As you have read, Americans rely heavily on the news media to reduce the amount of unethical behavior by government officials. What do you see as potential strengths and weaknesses of this reliance on the news media?

Strengths

_____

_____

_____

Weaknesses

_____

_____

_____

For each of the following statements, circle a number to indicate how strongly you agree or disagree, then explain why you think so.

Critical Thinking Exercise 6E, Page 105

1. **Government "by the people" requires that the people use wisdom.**

| STRONGLY AGREE | 1 | 2 | 3 | 4 | 5 | STRONGLY DISAGREE |

_____

_____

_____

_____

2. Only those citizens who vote have a right to complain about the way the government operates.

STRONGLY AGREE	1	2	3	4	5	STRONGLY DISAGREE

_____

_____

_____

_____

3. It is unrealistic for citizen-leaders to expect that their representatives agree with them on every issue. It is very realistic to demand that those representatives should act with honesty, integrity, and honor.

STRONGLY AGREE	1	2	3	4	5	STRONGLY DISAGREE

_____

_____

_____

_____

4. Most people get the kind of government that they deserve.

STRONGLY AGREE	1	2	3	4	5	STRONGLY DISAGREE

_____

_____

_____

_____

1. Write several rules that you think should be part of a code of ethics for government officials and employees in your community.

_____

_____

_____

_____

_____

_____

2. Choose one of the following ethical scandals, or people associated with potential ethical scandals, from American history. Research your topic, answer the questions provided, and share your findings with the class.

Matthew Lyon (1790s)

William "Boss" Tweed and Tammany Hall (1860s)

The attempt to impeach Andrew Johnson (1860s)

The Congressional "salary grab" (1870s)

Credit Mobilier (1870s)

John D. Sanborn (1870s)

William W. Belknap (1870s)

Teapot Dome Scandal (1920s)

Spiro Agnew (1970s)

Watergate (1970s)

Savings & Loan Crisis (1980s)

"Keating Five" (1980s)

Iran-Contra Arms Scandal (1980s)

House Bank Scandal (1990s)

House Post Office Scandal (1990s)

a. **Briefly describe the facts of the scandal. (Who was involved? What did they do? Why?)**

_____

_____

_____

_____

b. **What did the people involved in the scandal do that was ethically wrong, or perceived to be ethically wrong?**

_____

_____

_____

_____

c. **What were some of the consequences of the scandal for the people involved in it and for the nation?**

_____

_____

_____

_____

d. **What role did the press or the news media play in how America found out about the potentially unethical actions?**

_____

_____

_____

_____

ETHICS AND NEW TECHNOLOGIES

OBJECTIVES

After completing this chapter, you will be able to:

■ 1. Identify current ethical issues in computer technology.

■ 2. Apply critical thinking skills to ethical questions relevant to computer technology.

■ 3. Describe guidelines for the ethical use of computer technology.

■ Focus

Bill Byte is in his first year of teaching computer classes at Abe Lincoln High School. He has been frustrated because the school's computer labs are stocked with old, nearly obsolete software. Last month, Bill ran across a computer magazine article about MegaTeach, a new tutorial program. The article said that MegaTeach was the best software ever written for teaching high school students how to use computers. Although MegaTeach was very expensive ($300 per copy), Bill decided to order it for himself, sacrificing some of the money he had been saving for a new car.

When Bill tried out MegaTeach at home, he found it was every bit as good as the article had said. In his excitement, Bill showed the article and his copy of the software to his friend Arlene, a math teacher at Lincoln. Her reaction was discouraging. "Bill," said Arlene, "there are 20 computers in your lab. Buying this software for each of them would cost $6,000! The school can't afford to spend that kind of money right now. The school already has to buy new band uniforms and resurface the gym floor this year. If you request MegaTeach today, you won't get funding for a year or two! Why don't you order it now and just make 20 copies of your disk to use until the school buys legal copies? Don't tell anyone, but that's how I got the WhizMath computer software for my classes."

That night, Bill sat at his kitchen table thinking about his dilemma. His students really needed MegaTeach. But by the time the school could afford to buy it, MegaTeach might be obsolete. Making the copies would be easy, but would it be right? The copyright statement on the software clearly said, "If MegaTeach is used on multiple computers, a separate copy of the software must be purchased for each computer used."

1. If Bill came to you for advice, what would you suggest that he do? Why?

_____

_____

_____

_____

2. List several ethical issues or questions that you see in this case study.

_____

_____

_____

3. List several other ethical issues or questions faced by people using computers at their schools, homes, or jobs.

_____

_____

_____

_____

■ The Exploding Growth of New Technologies

In July 1994, America celebrated the 25th anniversary of the Apollo 11 space flight. This mission marked the first time that humans walked on the surface of the moon, one of the most important events of the 20th century. Space flights like Apollo 11 could not have been accomplished without major innovations in computer engineering and technology. Yet the computers and software programs used by NASA in the 1960s and 70s are considered primitive today. Many home computer systems are, pound for pound, far more sophisticated and powerful than the computers and software used by the Apollo astronauts to get to the moon and back!

We live in a time of exploding growth in new technologies. These inventions and ideas can help people solve difficult problems, but they also seem to raise hosts of new ethical questions. In this chapter, you will investigate several ethical issues, questions, and problems associated with computers and new technologies.

■ New Technology: Patterns in Human History

Throughout history, advances in technology have often helped people to be more productive and to improve the quality of their lives. The earliest technological advances, such as the use of metals and the inventions of the wheel and tools, made it possible for humans to survive in a hostile environment. Later technologies, such as electricity, telephones, automobiles, and airplanes, made life more convenient and brought people from distant places together. Throughout human history, several patterns have emerged in the relationship between people, ethics, and new technologies.

One pattern has been that humans seem to have a love/hate relationship with new technologies. People seem both excited about a technology's potential for good and frightened of its unknown consequences. However, in spite of our fears, once new technologies are visualized, they almost always get produced. For example, humans envisioned "horseless carriages" and "flying machines" many years before automobiles and airplanes were invented. It was understood by a few that the ability to transport people to distant places quickly would be essential as new societies sprang up around the globe. Many more people were simply excited by the romance and adventure of traveling to new lands. However, some early skeptics of trains and automobiles warned that traveling at such high speeds would damage people's internal organs. In the end, of course, trains and automobiles were built anyway, and the skeptics were quieted by reality.

Another pattern is that it is only *after* new technologies are introduced into a society that the ethical implications of the technologies are well understood. For example, early researchers into the nature of the atom suspected that their findings would revolutionize life on earth. However, there was no way they could have known all of the ethical questions that this research would later raise.

A third pattern in human history is that the more potential that new technologies have to be used for good purposes, the more potential they also have to be used in ways that are harmful. Airplanes, for example, have helped humans see past their national, racial, and geographic barriers to better understand the common traits that we all share. On the other hand, airplanes also helped usher in modern warfare, in which millions of civilians have been killed through air raids and bombings. Like all other technologies, airplanes are not good or bad in themselves. It is how they are used that can be considered right or wrong.

A fourth and somewhat surprising pattern is that new technologies do not really produce new ethical issues at all. Instead, these innovations simply force people to look at *old* ethical issues in new ways. After all, humans had been wrestling with the ethics of war long before airplanes were invented. And people were concerned about an individual's right to privacy long before computers were added to that discussion.

"I think that if you could take the best of the ethics of yesterday and mix it with the ethics of today when it is at its best, then it would be something very fine." (Astrid Lindgren)

CRITICAL THINKING

To further analyze historical patterns in the relationship between people and technology, complete Critical Thinking Exercise 7A on pages 127-128.

■ Ethical Hot Spots in Computer Technology

There are many ethical issues relevant to computer technology. In this section you will read about a few specific issues that are especially important and controversial today. Try to understand not just the main ethical issues, but also the many other ethical questions that are behind the main issues. This practice of reading between the lines is a good way to sharpen your critical thinking skills by applying the Critical Thinking model from Chapter 4.

UNETHICAL SOFTWARE COPYING AND PIRACY

Computer software is simply information stored on a special type of disk. This information—like the information in books, videotapes, musical tapes, and CDs—is easily copied. (See Illustration 7-1.) This copying is necessary for software customers to be able to transfer the information onto their computer hard drives and to make backup copies in case something goes wrong. However, some computer users take unfair advantage of this system by copying someone else's software instead of buying it themselves.

Illustration 7-1

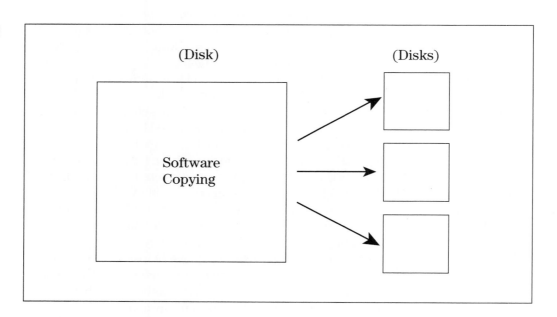

In extreme cases, this copying can lead to software piracy. (See Illustration 7-2.) **Software piracy** is the act of making many copies of a disk and then selling the copies for much less than the software's retail price. Software authors and publishers argue that copying and piracy are both forms of stealing. They wrote and marketed the programs, so they are entitled to the profits. On the other hand, some copiers claim that software companies charge too much for their products and that the information on the disks should be available to everyone. As a critical thinker, which argument do you think is stronger? Why?

> "One of the greatest pains to human nature is the pain of a new idea." (Walter Bagehot)

Illustration 7-2

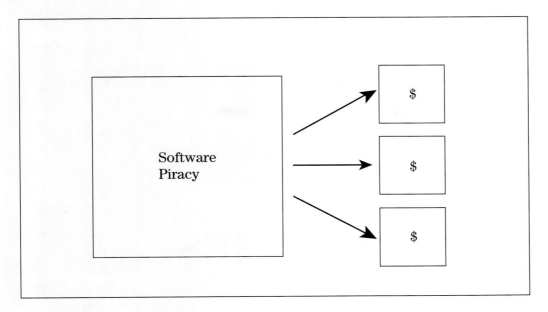

HACKING AND VIRUSES

In computer jargon, **hacking** is the act of using one's own computer equipment to "break into" the computer system of others and find information. *Hackers* use computers and *modems* as tools to "get inside" other computers. Critics of hacking say that it is like walking through a neighborhood and checking every door and window of every house to see if any were left unlocked. When an unlocked door or window is found, the hackers enter and look through the owners' belongings.

Even if no property is damaged, such behavior would still show blatant disregard for the rights of others. However, hackers maintain that, if computers without security systems are like houses left with the front doors open, then perhaps the "victims" deserve what they get. Many hackers view hacking more as a harmless game of trying to beat computer security programs. As hackers become more skilled at getting into computer systems, the owners of the systems create better security measures to keep the hackers out. In fact, many former amateur hackers now design computer security systems for a living. Which point of view do you think is backed up by stronger arguments? Why?

Hacking takes on more sinister implications when it is tied to the spread of computer viruses. (See Illustration 7-3.) **Computer viruses** are programs that are designed to damage or negatively affect other computers, usually by causing the loss of information. Viruses represent high-tech vandalism. These computer viruses are often spread by hiding them in other programs. The other programs are put onto computers, either by inserting disks or by using modems. The viruses go along for the ride and begin to spread and do their damage. Computer owners can buy security programs that find and get rid of viruses, but new viruses are currently being created at a faster pace than the security programs can match. Which ethical principles are violated by the intentional spread of computer viruses? Would any ethical principles permit it?

> "In the 21st century, survival will be a more complicated and precarious question than ever before, and the ethics required of us must be correspondingly sophisticated." (Oscar Arias)

Illustration 7-3

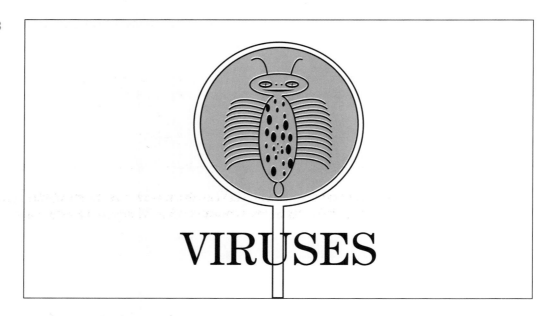

VIRUSES

INVASION OF PRIVACY

Some of the more frightening aspects of recent computer technology have to do with people's privacy rights. Every time people use credit cards, file insurance claims, receive speeding tickets, or enter hospitals, personal information about those people is entered into computer databases. There are laws that should protect people from having that information used in unwanted or unfair ways. Unfortunately, these laws have not kept up with the advances in technology. Hospitals, for example, sometimes sell lists of names and addresses of new mothers to companies that sell baby products. In many states, such actions are legal, even without the patients' permission. Even more harm can be done when the stored information is not accurate. One recent study found that more than one-third of credit reports kept on Americans contained mistakes and inaccuracies.

Even when the businesses compiling the information are accurate and act ethically, computer hackers can often gain access to the information anyway. One college student hacker recently demonstrated this during a class presentation. After only a few hours of work with his home computer and modem, the student produced his teacher's address, phone number, social security number, "confidential" credit report, and driving record for the past five years. Protecting people's privacy will become even more difficult as the number of companies collecting and needing access to such information continues to increase.

ETHICS AND NETWORKING

Computer networks are among the newer advances in computer technology. (See Illustration 7-4.) *Networks* are complex systems of computers connected by modems and high-speed telephone lines. The largest computer network in the world is the Internet. The *Internet* is a massive worldwide web of connected computers. It was originally created (on a smaller scale) by the U. S. Department of Defense to keep our government agencies operating in the event of nuclear war or other national catastrophes. Having grown tremendously since its early days, the Internet represents the passing lane on the information superhighway. However, some critics charge that networks like the Internet are superhighways without police or even safe operating laws.

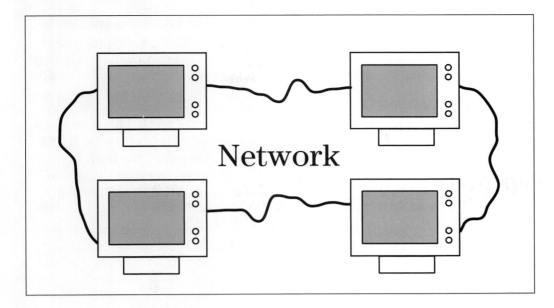

Illustration 7-4

Network

Some of the ethical problems already mentioned are even more relevant to computer networks. Viruses can be easily reproduced and spread to thousands of networked computers. Software can be illegally copied and distributed to many computers at once. Individual privacy can be even harder to protect as networked hackers gain access to more computers.

There are also several ethical issues that apply more specifically to computer networks. One example is censorship. Some areas of the Internet, designed for adult-only use, contain pornographic pictures and erotic writing. Few effective safeguards have even been put into place to restrict the access of children to these areas. What ethical principles can you think of that might relate to the issue of restricting children's access to pornographic materials?

Also, some users of networks have been harassed, tormented, and even stalked by others. Many critics charge that the administrators of the computer networks have not acted forcefully enough to prevent these types of abuses. Administrators respond by saying that their role, like that of the postal service, is to keep the system working and the information moving. They argue that there is little they can do to control what one individual says to another.

> "We cannot live happily as human beings in the belief that our own actions don't matter."
> (Alvin Toffler)

CRITICAL THINKING

It is your turn to apply critical thinking skills to one of the controversial ethical issues in computer technology. Turn to Critical Thinking Exercise 7B on pages 128 and 129.

■ Ethical Guidelines For Computer Use

As mentioned earlier, it is typical for technology to progress at a faster pace than the corresponding ethical discussions. The advancement of computer technology has certainly followed that pattern. Although there have been a few attempts at creating one, there is no universally accepted code of ethics for computer users or computer professionals. However, many people involved in computer technology are starting to openly discuss the need for such a code, or at least for some basic ethical guidelines.

There is no reason to believe that the ethical principles that we use to find answers to other moral dilemmas can't apply to computer technology as well. As you have already seen, new technologies do not really produce new ethical problems, just new ways of looking at familiar problems. Therefore, the heart of a computer code of ethics would need to include guidelines based on the ethical principles of *consequences, virtues, rights,* and *duties.* (See Illustration 7-5.)

Illustration 7-5

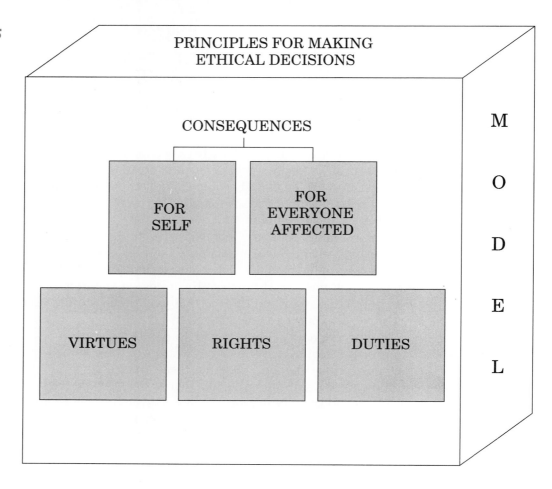

PRINCIPLES FOR MAKING
ETHICAL DECISIONS

CONSEQUENCES

FOR
SELF

FOR
EVERYONE
AFFECTED

VIRTUES   RIGHTS   DUTIES

M O D E L

Remember that the consequential approach to ethics includes the principles of egoism and utility. The principle of *egoism* states that the right thing for a person to do in any situation is the action that best serves that person's own long-term best interests. The principle of *utility* states that the morally right action is the one that produces the best consequences for everyone involved, not just for one individual. It would seem logical, then, that an effective computer code of ethics would include rules against the intentional spread of computer viruses, since that would promote better consequences for everyone involved. In addition, an effective computer code of ethics would need to make it clear that it is in each computer user's best interests to follow the rules. Like many corporate and professional codes of ethics, a computer code of ethics might include punishments for violations.

The principle of *virtues* states that ethics should be based on ideal character traits that people should try to incorporate into their lives. These virtues include ideals such as honesty, loyalty, respect, and responsibility. A computer ethical guideline based on respect would prohibit the practice of harassing others through computer networks, since doing so shows disrespect.

The principle of *rights* states that people should respect the rights of others. Remember that a right refers to how an individual is entitled to be treated by others. One way a computer code of ethics could promote this principle would be by limiting how corporations can use personal information and with whom they can share it. Such rules protect people's right to privacy.

The principle of *duties* states that ethics should be based on fulfilling one's moral obligations to others. There are many interpretations of what people's ethical duties are, but one good example is Immanuel Kant's principle of universality. As discussed in Chapter 2, *universality* is the idea that people should act as they would want others to act in the same kind of situation. A computer ethics guideline based on universality would forbid the copying and pirating of software. After all, if you were the author of the software, wouldn't you want to be fairly paid for your work?

CRITICAL THINKING

You can try your hand at writing a code of ethics for computer users. Complete Critical Thinking Exercise 7C on page 130.

"Man has mounted science, and is now runaway... Some day science may have the existence of man in its power, and the human race may commit suicide by blowing up the world." (Henry Adams)

Remember, this section is reserved for you to write about your personal thoughts and feelings. You will not be expected to turn in these answers or share them with others.

1. Read the case study about Bill Byte again (pages 113-114). Do you think it would be unethical for Bill to copy the MegaTeach program to use in his classes? Why?

_____

_____

2. Look at your answer to Question #1 on page 114. After reading the chapter, would you still give the same advice to Bill? If not, explain why you changed your mind.

_____

_____

3. Journal.

   a. One interesting thing that I learned in this chapter was:

   _____

   _____

   b. One aspect of computer ethics that I would like to learn more about is:

   _____

   _____

   c. After reading this chapter, I am planning to make the following changes in the way I use computers:

   _____

   _____

1. **Besides computers, give one example of a new type of technology that seems to fit each of the following historical patterns. You can use your own knowledge, library resources, or interviews with others to find answers.**

    a. **People have a love/hate relationship with new technologies. People seem both excited about a technology's potential for good and frightened of its unknown consequences.**

    _____

    _____

    b. **It is only *after* new technologies are introduced into a society that the ethical implications of the technologies are well understood.**

    _____

    _____

    c. **The more potential that new technologies have to be used for good purposes, the more potential they also have to be used in ways that are harmful.**

    _____

    _____

    d. **New technologies do not really produce new ethical issues at all, but simply force people to look at old ethical issues in new ways.**

    _____

    _____

2. **Write one way that the relationship between people and computers fits each of the following historical patterns. (Use your own original examples, not the ones mentioned in the chapter.)**

    a. **People have a love/hate relationship with new technologies. People seem both excited about a technology's potential for good and frightened of its unknown consequences.**

    _____

    _____

b. It is only *after* new technologies are introduced into a society that the ethical implications of the technologies are well understood.

_____

_____

c. The more potential that new technologies have to be used for good purposes, the more potential they also have to be used in ways that are harmful.

_____

_____

d. New technologies do not really produce new ethical issues at all, but simply force people to look at old ethical issues in new ways.

_____

_____

Critical Thinking Exercise 7B, Page 121

Choose one of the hot spot *ethical issues mentioned in the chapter. Then use your critical thinking skills to learn more about the issue and find answers to the ethical questions involved.*

Ethical Issues (choose one):

a. Software copying

b. Software piracy

c. Hacking

d. Viruses

e. Individual privacy rights

f. Network issue: protecting children vs. censorship

g. Network issue: harassing others

Critical Thinking Model:

Step 1: Clearly state the ethical question under consideration.

_____

_____

Step 2: Research to find the information you need. (List possible sources of information here.)

_____

_____

Step 3: Identify possible answers to the ethical question.

a. _____

_____

b. _____

_____

c. _____

_____

d. _____

_____

Step 4: Evaluate the strengths and weaknesses of each possible answer. (Remember to look for fallacies and ethical principles that could apply.)

<u>**Strengths**</u>   <u>**Weaknesses**</u>

a. _____   _____

_____   _____

b. _____   _____

_____   _____

c. _____   _____

_____   _____

d. _____   _____

_____   _____

Step 5: Choose the best answer and be able to defend it.

_____

_____

1. **What rules or guidelines do you think should be included in a code of ethics for computer users? Write two rules or guidelines that are relevant to each of the following ethical principles.**

a. **The principle of egoism**

_____

_____

b. **The principle of utility**

_____

_____

c. **The principle of virtues**

_____

_____

d. **The principle of rights**

_____

_____

e. **The principle of duties**

_____

_____

1. **Watch for references to computer ethics in the news media. Notice which ethical issues are being discussed. Also note any references to ethical principles, ethical guidelines, or laws that apply to these issues.**

2. **Interview several people you know who use computers regularly at home or at work. What computer-related ethical issues do they think are the most important? What do they think about the code of ethics you wrote in Critical Thinking Exercise 7C?**

BIOETHICS

OBJECTIVES

After completing this chapter, you will be able to:

■   1.   Define basic terms relevant to bioethics.

■   2.   Describe various categories of euthanasia.

■   3.   Identify key ethical questions in the euthanasia debate.

■   4.   Identify ethical questions relevant to genetic engineering.

■   5.   Apply critical thinking skills to specific bioethical issues.

■ Focus

Crystal sat quietly in her easy chair, thumbing through the packet of forms from the doctor's office. She and her husband, Bob, had decided to have a baby this year, and they had many decisions to make. Form #1 asked for the child's birthday. Crystal wrote July 25, 2058. One of the advantages of Genetic Engineered Reproduction (GER) was being able to pick any birth date you wanted. To Crystal, the biggest advantage was that the process eliminated all known birth defects. Form #2 was the Genetic Menu. For "sex," Crystal checked "female," proud that she had won that argument with Bob. Under "physical traits," she checked the boxes for blonde hair, blue eyes, and a medium-thin body type. Crystal ordered a mix of Swedish and Scottish facial features. West African and Latin were more popular choices this year, but she wanted the child to reflect her and Bob's family histories. After Crystal noted her preferences for final height (5'8"), intelligence (150 IQ), and specific talents (music, physical coordination, and science), she went on to Form #3.

This form explained some of Crystal's other medical options. Did she wish that medications previously tested on animals be given to her and the baby? In the event of a technical error, did Crystal and Bob want to have an abortion? If so, did they wish to donate fetal tissue for medical research? Should the worst happen, which drug did Crystal prefer to be used for her euthanasia? And, of course, with which credit card would she be paying?

After completing all of the forms, Crystal scanned her answers into her computer and electronically mailed the packet back to the doctor's office. Having a baby was so exciting! For a moment she wondered how mothers-to-be in the past had felt, not knowing how their babies would turn out. It was hard to imagine leaving the welfare and health of her baby up to a genetic roll of the dice. Medical science had made having a baby so much simpler!

WHAT DO YOU THINK?

1. Write down as many ethical issues or questions as you can find in the case study.

_____

_____

2. What parts of the story seem the most far fetched to you? Why?

_____

_____

3. What parts of the story make you the most uncomfortable? Why?

_____

_____

4. What other ethical issues can you think of that are related to medicine, medical technology, or health care?

_____

_____

BIOETHICS

"The essence of ethics is some level of caring." (Michael Josephson)

Bioethics is the study of ethical issues related to medicine and health. More than a decade ago, sociologists were predicting that by the early 1990s, bioethics would produce the most controversial ethical debates in America. With current debates raging over bioethical issues such as abortion, euthanasia, nationwide health care coverage, and genetic engineering, those forecasts seem to be coming true. As Crystal's story illustrates, there are many important bioethical issues and questions. In this chapter you will explore two of those issues more closely, euthanasia and genetic engineering.

■ Euthanasia

Euthanasia is killing that is done in the victim's best interests, usually to relieve intense suffering. The term originates from two Greek words, *eu* (pronounced *hue*), meaning "good, pleasant, or happy," and *thanatos,* meaning "death." However, that is a translation, not a definition. The pleasantness of a death is not what qualifies it as euthanasia. Rather, it is the intent behind the act itself.

LIMITING THE SCOPE OF THE DISCUSSION

The term *euthanasia* only applies to situations in which death is considered to be in the best interests of the patient or victim. When people are killed for the benefit of others, it is considered to be homicide or murder. In the case of euthanasia, it is often the victims or patients who make the determination for themselves that death is in their best interests, but not always. As you will see, there are times when the decision must be made by others. So if a man kills his ailing aunt out of compassion to end her suffering, it is euthanasia. Killing her to get a large inheritance or because he is tired of caring for her may be murder, but it is certainly not euthanasia.

Simply claiming that a killing fits the definition of euthanasia does not, in itself, make the act morally right. The possible morality of euthanasia depends on other factors as well. For example, *euthanizing* sick or injured animals has different ethical implications than euthanizing people. With human euthanasia, some medical ethicists argue that the most important factor is how the victim or patient dies. Others claim that the primary key is what the victim or patient wants. In the following section you will see how those two important issues produce different categories of euthanasia.

> "Once again, the patient does not know whether the approaching physician is coming in the guise of healer or killer." (Margaret Mead)

CRITICAL THINKING

To analyze some of the ethical issues raised by euthanasia, complete Critical Thinking Exercise 8A on page 141.

CATEGORIES OF EUTHANASIA

Every euthanasia situation is unique. That fact makes it difficult to argue that euthanasia is *always* right or *always* wrong. Instead, euthanasia cases are usually categorized according to four key concepts: voluntary, nonvoluntary, active, and passive.

- **Voluntary euthanasia** requires that a victim be mentally competent and desire to die.

- **Nonvoluntary euthanasia** means that the victim is not mentally capable of deciding what he or she wants. This mental impairment could be caused by a long-term coma, a severe stroke, or a disease such as Alzheimer's.

- **Active euthanasia** is used to describe a situation in which a suffering person is intentionally killed. Methods of active euthanasia have included drug overdoses, shootings, and suffocation.

- **Passive euthanasia** refers to situations in which the victim is not killed, but merely *allowed to die* by withholding medical treatments. A common example of passive euthanasia would be when life support machines are disconnected from the body of a dying person.

Combining these four concepts in differing ways makes it possible to divide euthanasia cases into four distinct categories (See Illustration 8-1):

- *Voluntary active* cases would include mentally capable victims wishing to die, who either kill themselves or are killed by others. When terminally ill people choose to kill themselves, or have others kill them, it is considered voluntary active euthanasia.

- *Voluntary passive* cases of euthanasia require that victims be mentally competent and choose to have life-sustaining medical treatments withheld from themselves. These patients often express their wishes in living wills. A living will is a legal document that places limits on the types of life-sustaining medical procedures that people wish to receive once they can no longer express their wishes.

- *Nonvoluntary active* cases are those in which the victims are not mentally capable of making decisions for themselves, so others make the decision to kill them to end their suffering. An example would be a long-term coma victim who is given a fatal drug overdose.

- *Nonvoluntary passive* cases occur when victims who are not capable of deciding their own fates have life-sustaining medical treatments withheld to hasten their deaths. A common example would be when medical workers disconnect life-support equipment from a dying person who is no longer conscious.

Illustration 8-1

Subject is Mentally Competent
and Wishes to Die

Voluntary Active	Voluntary Passive
Nonvoluntary Active	Nonvoluntary Passive

Subject is Killed

Subject is Allowed to Die

Subject is Not
Mentally Competent

CRITICAL THINKING

Demonstrate that you understand the differences in the four categories of euthanasia. Complete Critical Thinking Exercise 8B on page 141.

THE LEGAL STATUS OF EUTHANASIA

American laws regulating the practice of euthanasia have been changing since the early 1970s. It was then that the first court order permitting euthanasia was granted, in the highly controversial (nonvoluntary passive) case of Karen Quinlan. Over the years, passive euthanasia cases (both voluntary and nonvoluntary) have become much more common across the country. Many hospitals now routinely require patients to fill out *living wills* clearly stating their wishes regarding life-sustaining medical procedures. However, even though most Americans now seem to be less offended by passive euthanasia cases, the ethical and legal controversies behind euthanasia have not subsided. The debates have simply shifted to the questions raised by active euthanasia, currently illegal across America.

Federal and state laws against killing others do not make exceptions for cases in which the killing is done with the victims' consent or for their own good. However, pro-euthanasia, "right-to-die" groups are now challenging some of those laws in the courts. No matter which side of this legal debate wins, remember that a legal standard and a moral standard are not the same. The question of whether or not active euthanasia should be legally allowed is very different from whether it is morally right or wrong.

ARGUMENTS AGAINST THE MORALITY OF ACTIVE EUTHANASIA

Intentionally killing others violates the basic moral virtue of respect for human life. While people should have basic human rights and freedoms, these liberties do not include a "right to die." After all, our society does not give people the right to commit suicide. For example, some people want to die to escape intense pain. Pain, however, can—and should be— controlled through medication. Suffering people can be made more comfortable without killing them.

Finally, allowing active euthanasia could easily lead to abuses. After all, the definition of euthanasia is based as much on people's intentions as on their actions. How could a judge or jury know whether a wealthy, sick person was killed out of compassion or because the heirs were impatient to get an inheritance? What if legalizing active euthanasia led to policies like the ones Adolf Hitler used to kill thousands of mentally and physically impaired people "for the good of the state"?

ARGUMENTS FOR THE MORALITY OF ACTIVE EUTHANASIA

While respect for human life is important, the quality of human life matters, too. To some people, a life filled with suffering and misery may not be worth living. Pain is only one part of the issue. Even if pain can be limited, human dignity and the sense of control over one's life are still important issues. The moral principle of rights states that people have the freedom or liberty to do anything that does not violate the rights of others. These liberties should include the right to have some control over how and when one dies.

Finally, the arguments warning of potential abuses of active euthanasia are little more than scare tactics. Don't forget that opponents of the airplane, the television, and almost every other new idea in history also used slippery slope fallacies. They wanted people to think that these new ideas would lead to horrifying consequences, but that rarely happens. Active euthanasia should be carefully regulated to prevent abuses, but using fallacies designed to scare people does not help the debate.

> "The question is...whether we as a society stand ready to countenance the legalized killing of one person by another." (C. Everett Koop)

> "Today is a good day to die, for all the things of my life are present." (Chief Crazy Horse)

CRITICAL THINKING

Which set of arguments do you think is stronger? Apply your critical thinking skills to evaluate the preceding sets of arguments. Turn to Critical Thinking Exercise 8C on page 142.

◼ The Genetic Revolution

A second controversial issue in bioethics today has to do with research in the area of human genes. (See Illustration 8-2.) *Genes* are microscopic parts of chromosomes, which influence the inheritance and development of specific characteristics. Every cell in the human body contains millions of genes. Some of your genes determined your height, hair texture, foot size, and eye color long before you were born. Other genes determined whether or not you would be predisposed to allergies, ulcers, some mental illnesses, and hosts of other diseases and genetic disorders. Unlocking the mysteries within human genes is the next great frontier of medical research.

Illustration 8-2

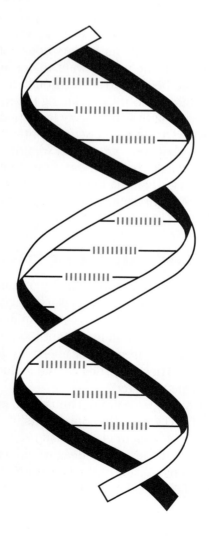

RECENT ADVANCES AND FUTURE CONCERNS

Genetic research is moving along faster than you may think. Medical researchers all over the globe are currently racing to create a map of all of the human genes and their locations on our chromosomes. This massive endeavor is called the Human Genome Project. Among the genes located so far is one thought to cause cystic fibrosis and others that predispose people to certain types of cancers. Once genes for these inherited problems are located and mapped, individuals can be tested to find out whether or not they are at risk to develop the disorders. Locating the genes that cause genetic disorders, however, is not the same as curing the disorders. Curing or "fixing" defective genes is the logical next step.

Every time the mappers locate a gene responsible for a disorder, other researchers rush in to learn how to fix that defective gene through genetic engineering. **Genetic engineering** is the process of creating genes that serve specific purposes. Early experiments in *genetic repair,* some performed on humans, have shown encouraging results. For example, two children with life-threatening genetic disorders of the immune system were given injections of healthy versions of the defective gene. The hope was that the healthy genes would replace the defective ones in the childrens' bodies. So far, researchers are cautiously optimistic that the procedures seem to be working. Some less-cautious medical experts are already claiming that if these *gene therapies* are successful, most genetic birth defects, handicaps, and genetically caused illnesses could be eliminated within a generation or two.

As you saw in Crystal's case study at the beginning of this chapter, genetic engineering has the potential to go one giant step further. Some critics argue that genetic repair will eventually lead to a kind of *genetic enhancement.* After all, if hereditary blindness is a birth defect that can be "cured," why not just give all children a gene for 20/20 vision? If facial deformities can be genetically repaired, why not give everyone genes for high, chiseled cheekbones and perfect noses? If a life span of 70 to 90 years is genetically programmed into our bodies, why not change the genetic program to 150 or 300 years?

Obviously, the dividing line between genetic repair and genetic enhancement is not as clear as it first appears. Obesity is one of the leading public health problems in America today. Suppose there is a gene that predisposes some people to obesity, as many researchers believe. Would it be wrong to routinely fix that gene in newborns or human embryos? Several arguments for and against this type of genetic engineering are presented in the following section. Use your critical thinking skills to analyze and evaluate the strengths and weaknesses of each set of arguments.

ARGUMENTS AGAINST AGGRESSIVE GENETIC ENGINEERING

Genetic engineering, whether by repairing birth defects or by ordering babies with the characteristics we want, is "playing God." Nature intends for all individuals to have some genetic imperfections. It is unfortunate that some individuals have very serious genetic defects, but that is how it was meant to be. Some human genes do seem to naturally evolve and change over time. (For example, people are generally taller now than they were several hundred years ago.) But it would be wrong, foolhardy, and dangerous to unnaturally accelerate this evolutionary process.

It is also likely that genetic engineering will cause unintended physical side effects. The invention of antibiotics such as penicillin has led to the evolution of super-bacteria that are increasingly resistant to antibiotics. The same thing could

"The only thing that makes life possible is permanent, intolerable uncertainty: not knowing what comes next." (Ursula K. Le Guin)

"Life consists, not in holding good cards, but in playing well those you hold." (Josh Billings)

easily happen with genetic engineering, leaving us with even bigger problems than we face now. For example, what if we find out that tinkering with one gene damages or weakens others? In addition, genetic engineering in humans will almost certainly also result in unintended emotional side effects. We may not enjoy our physical imperfections, but dealing with them throughout life and over-coming our natural limitations produces character and strength. If we take away the struggles that produce character, what kind of people will we become?

ARGUMENTS FOR AGGRESSIVE GENETIC ENGINEERING

"Adversity is the first path to truth."
(Lord Byron)

First, we should realize that all medical research represents an attempt to "play God." Every illness cured, every broken bone set, and every life saved is another small step in humanity's quest to conquer natural obstacles. Genetic engineering may represent a bigger step than some other medical technologies, but it isn't really different. With or without genetic engineering, human bodies may someday adapt to the point that cancers no longer plague us. So what's wrong with speeding up the process?

It is true that genetic engineering will probably produce unintended physical, emotional, and social effects. But it would be wrong to assume that all of these side effects will be negative. Money now spent on chronic health problems could be used for more fulfilling purposes. Longer, healthier lives will make humans more productive. Imagine the benefits humanity could have received if people such as Marie Curie, Albert Einstein, Sojourner Truth, Confucius, Elizabeth Barrett-Browning, or Booker T. Washington could have lived another fifty years!

While it is true that overcoming adversity builds character, serious genetic disorders are obstacles that many people find overwhelming. Some people may grow stronger because of these handicaps, but many more find their lives destroyed. Isn't it heartless to tell children suffering from genetic disorders that, while they could have lived normal, healthy lives, instead they will have to suffer in order to develop character?

CRITICAL THINKING

Evaluate the strengths and weaknesses of the preceding arguments by completing Critical Thinking Exercise 8D on page 143.

Applications

Remember that this section is reserved for you to write your personal views and opinions. You will not be expected to turn in these answers or share them with others.

1. Under what conditions, if any, do you think euthanasia would be morally right? Why? What moral principles support your view?

_____

_____

_____

_____

2. Under what conditions, if any, do you think euthanasia would be morally wrong? Why? What moral principles support your view?

_____

_____

_____

_____

3. What uses, if any, of genetic research and engineering do you think would be good or morally right? Why? What moral principles support your view?

_____

_____

_____

_____

4. What uses, if any, of genetic research and engineering do you think would be bad or morally wrong? Why? What moral principles support your view?

_____

_____

_____

_____

5. Journal.

    a. **One thing that I learned about euthanasia in this chapter is:**

_____

_____

    b. **One thing that I learned about genetic research is:**

_____

_____

    c. **One thing in this chapter that I disagreed with is:**

_____

_____

1. **Write an example of a situation involving the killing of a person that would fit the definition of euthanasia given in this chapter.**

Critical Thinking Exercise 8A, Page 133

2. **Write an example of a situation involving the killing of a person that would not fit the definition of euthanasia given in this chapter.**

Give one original example for each of the four categories of euthanasia discussed in the text.

Critical Thinking Exercise 8B, Page 134

1. **Voluntary Active Euthanasia**

2. **Voluntary Passive Euthanasia**

3. **Nonvoluntary Active Euthanasia**

4. **Nonvoluntary Passive Euthanasia**

1. **Step 4 in the Critical Thinking Model is to evaluate the strengths and weaknesses of arguments on both sides of an ethical debate. Apply your knowledge of ethical principles, fallacies, and even common sense to the arguments given in the text.**

Arguments *Against* the Morality of Active Euthanasia:

Strengths_____

_____

_____

Weaknesses_____

_____

_____

Arguments *for* the Morality of Active Euthanasia:

Strengths_____

_____

_____

Weaknesses_____

_____

_____

2. **List several arguments against and for the morality of active euthanasia that were not mentioned in the text. Good sources of information would include newspaper and magazine articles, encyclopedias, and interviews with medical workers and with people who have experienced life-threatening illnesses in their families.**

Additional Arguments Against the Morality of Active Euthanasia

_____

_____

_____

Additional Arguments for the Morality of Active Euthanasia

_____

_____

_____

1. **Evaluate the strengths and weaknesses of the arguments against and for aggressive genetic engineering. Apply your knowledge of ethical principles, fallacies, and even common sense to the arguments given in the text.**

Arguments *Against* Aggressive Genetic Engineering:

Strengths _____

_____

_____

Weaknesses _____

_____

_____

Arguments *for* Aggressive Genetic Engineering:

Strengths _____

_____

_____

Weaknesses _____

_____

_____

2. **List several arguments against and for the morality of aggressive genetic engineering that were not mentioned in the text. Good sources of information would include newspaper and magazine articles, encyclopedias, and interviews with medical workers and with people who have experienced genetic disorders in their families.**

Additional Arguments Against Aggressive Genetic Engineering:

_____

_____

_____

Additional Arguments for Aggressive Genetic Engineering:

_____

_____

_____

1. **Paraphrase the meanings of the following terms from this chapter. What do the words and phrases mean to you?**

   a. **Euthanasia** _____

   _____

   b. **Voluntary euthanasia** _____

   _____

   c. **Nonvoluntary euthanasia** _____

   _____

   d. **Active euthanasia** _____

   _____

   e. **Passive euthanasia** _____

   _____

   f. **Living will** _____

   _____

   g. **Genetic engineering** _____

   _____

2. *Conduct a mock jury trial based on the following active euthanasia case study. You and your classmates can play the roles of the family members, Dr. Gurney, the judge, the bailiff, the defense attorneys, the prosecuting attorneys, jurors, and any other expert witnesses that you wish to use. Have the attorneys call their witnesses and make their best cases to the jurors. Then, just as in a real trial, let the jury decide its verdict.*

CASE STUDY

Lou Hansen was once a famous brain surgeon and a professor at a leading medical school. He lived with his wife, Sue, and their teenage children, Terry (18) and Sherry (16), in an affluent neighborhood near Dallas. But everything changed a year ago when an artery burst in Lou's brain. As a result of the massive stroke, Lou is now totally paralyzed on his right side. He cannot speak and does not seem to comprehend what is said to him. Lou cannot feed, clothe, or clean himself, thus requiring round-the-clock care. Lou's doctor, Latricia Gurney,

told Sue that Lou was probably not feeling pain, but that he would never again be able to function mentally at an adult human level. Dr. Gurney added that Lou could live another 20 or 30 years.

Last week Sue found Lou's old personal journal in a desk drawer. She read through it, crying as she remembered the life she and her husband had once enjoyed. One entry, written three months before Lou's stroke, stopped her cold. In discussing his feelings about euthanasia, Lou had written, "I don't really fear death. What I fear most is losing my abilities to think, feel, work, and do the things I most enjoy in life. If this ever happens to me, I hope my family will have the courage and love to help me die. Such a miserable existence is not a life at all!"

That evening, Sue showed the journal entry to Terry and Sherry. They talked for hours about what they should do. Since Lou was not receiving any life-sustaining medical treatments, active euthanasia was the only way he could die. The family members knew that if they did that, one or more of them could end up in prison. The group finally went to bed with the dilemma still unresolved. At some time during the night, Terry went alone to Lou's room and suffocated him with a plastic bag. The next day Terry was charged with first degree murder in the death of his father.

3. Read the active euthanasia case study in the preceding exercise. Write a 500-word paper arguing that killing Mr. Hansen was either morally right or morally wrong. Your paper does not have to reflect your true feelings and opinions about the case. Just try to put together strong, consistent arguments on one side or the other. You are encouraged to back up your arguments with research sources such as books and magazine articles.

4. Survey people at your school, asking them what they think about euthanasia and genetic engineering. Remember to make your questions specific, since people can be in favor of one category of euthanasia or one use of genetic engineering, but against others.

ETHICS AND CULTURAL DIVERSITY

OBJECTIVES

After completing this chapter, you will be able to:

■ 1. Define key ethical terms relevant to cultural diversity.

■ 2. Explain strengths and weaknesses in the ways Americans have responded to cultural diversity in the past.

■ 3. Identify areas of similarity among people who seem different on the surface.

■ 4. Describe techniques for dealing with differences between people.

■ 5. Apply critical thinking skills to ethical issues relative to cultural diversity.

■ Focus

Every person you meet is the same as you in some ways and different from you in other ways. The following exercise will help consider some of these similarities and differences.

THE HUMAN SCAVENGER HUNT

Like a regular scavenger hunt, the goal of this exercise is to find all of the objects on the list. What's different about this *human* scavenger hunt is that the objects you are searching for are the names of people that fit each of the statements. Use each name only once. Don't use your own name.

1. _____ One of my parents or grandparents was born in another country.

2. _____ I think my name is unusual, but I like it.

3. _____ There is at least one way that I am like everyone else in this class.

4. _____ I have a skill or talent that I think is unique.

5. _____ I think that people like me are sometimes not treated fairly by others.

6. _____ I think that there is too much hatred, prejudice, and discrimination in our society.

7. _____ I think of myself as being open-minded and fair to others.

8. _____ I have at least one friend who is very different from me.

9. _____ There is at least one way in which I am different from everyone else in this class.

10. _____ I wish people would be more tolerant and accepting of others who are different from them.

11. _____ Sometimes I get tired of trying to fit in and be like everybody else.

12. _____ I think that a community or society gains strength by having different cultural, racial, and religious groups within it.

PEOPLE ARE DIFFERENT

The lesson of the scavenger hunt is that there are some characteristics that you share with many people and others that make you unique. This simple fact of life does not seem like it should cause much interference in our relationships with others, but it appears to. In spite of all of humanity's advancements in science, technology, and medicine, sometimes it seems as if people themselves are not advancing very much at all. News reports show us a world so often dominated by stories of war, violence, and hatred. And even America, founded on the belief that all people are created equal, has had a hard time living up to that belief. In this chapter, you will explore some of the ethical issues related to cultural diversity. You will learn strategies that will help you better understand, accept, and perhaps even admire people who are different from you.

■ Cultural Diversity: America's Checkered History

Cultural diversity refers to the fact that the world is comprised of many distinct and unique ethnic, racial, and religious groups. (See Illustration 9-1.) Thus, cultural diversity is not right or wrong, but simply a fact of life. Ethical questions about right or wrong can be asked, however, about how people respond to cultural differences.

Illustration 9-1

Regarding efforts to deal with cultural diversity, American history contains examples of the good, the bad, and the truly ugly.

THE GOOD

America began, in part, as a refuge for people who wanted to escape discrimination and make a better life. All cultural groups in the United States, including Native Americans, have ancestors who immigrated to North America from some other part of the world. Most, but not all, came voluntarily. Most of the early immigrants came to America for the same reasons that people still come today: for religious and political freedom, to escape poverty, for the adventure of staking their claim in a new world, and to give their children opportunities for a better life. As a result, America quickly established itself as a nation dedicated to making cultural diversity work.

Symbols of this culturally diverse heritage are all around us. American money is minted and printed with the motto *E PLURIBUS UNUM,* meaning "out of many, one." Our history books speak of great heroes and leaders—men and women—from every race, religion, and ethnic group in the land. The Statue of Liberty, donated by the nation of France in 1884, was intended to symbolize this unique characteristic of America. The inscription on the statue reads:

> *"Give me your tired, your poor,*
> *Your huddled masses yearning to breathe free,*
> *The wretched refuse of your teeming shore;*
> *I lift my lamp beside your golden door."*

Thus, much of what is best about America is expressed in our national values about diversity and tolerance. America was founded on a social philosophy that included the beliefs that:

- All persons are created equal.

- All persons have equal rights to life, liberty, and the pursuit of happiness.

- Every voice—no matter in what language it speaks—has a right to be heard.

- Unity does not come from uniformity, but from mutual respect and common interests.

THE BAD

While America has often been praised for its lofty values and beliefs, its citizens have at times been justly accused of hypocrisy. Those lofty principles have been

"Everybody—I don't care what color, creed, ethnic origin their roots are— we're all the same. We all have common roots. In spite of all of these technological achievements, we're beginning to understand there is a oneness to the whole universe— there is a oneness." (Reuben Snake)

hard to live up to. Americans have sometimes fallen into the trap of being selective about to whom those principles of equality and fairness apply. For example, each new wave of immigrants has faced discrimination and prejudice from other groups who got here first. At times, America's legal definition of a "person" has been based, for all practical purposes, on light skin color. Since only *persons* were assumed to have rights, this made it easier to justify social policies that violated the rights of minority groups such as Native Americans and African-Americans.

THE TRULY UGLY

The false assumption that some cultural and racial groups were less than human has had appalling effects. A striking example is slavery. Americans did not invent the practice of slavery, but we developed it into a national industry. Today, looking at sleepy town squares throughout the South, it seems almost inconceivable that only a few generations ago human beings were chained, sold, bought, and owned there by other human beings. But they were. And while slavery was practiced predominantly in the South, many Northerners supported the institution through their silence and through trade with the South. Thomas Jefferson, a slave-owner himself, predicted that slavery would end up destroying the new republic. It almost did, and the country's wounds are still not fully healed.

Other groups have faced persecution in America, too. Native American tribes were once the targets of a national policy that bordered on *genocide,* the annihilation of a race or cultural group. Also, thousands of American citizens had their possessions confiscated and found themselves and their families forced into American concentration camps during World War II. Their only crime was that they, their parents, or their grandparents had been born in Japan. Many Americans jumped to the hasty conclusion that, because these citizens *looked* Japanese, they were threats to America's national security.

Of course, the United States has not had a monopoly on prejudice, discrimination, and intolerance. These attitudes and practices have been universal throughout history. In fact, some people point out that, even when the worst American abuses are taken into account, cultural diversity has still worked better here than in most other nations. But critics argue that discrimination in America cannot be justified by claiming that someone else discriminated worse, for that would be a *two-wrongs-make-a-right* fallacy. If you found yourself in the cargo hold of a slave ship, being told that America's history of racial relationships has been better than average would not bring you much comfort.

CRITICAL THINKING

To further analyze and evaluate how Americans have dealt with cultural diversity throughout history, complete Critical Thinking Exercise 9A on page 157.

◼ Understanding Our Similarities

In a sense, the ethical debate over how people should deal with cultural diversity is one-sided. Few sane people would seriously argue that hate, discrimination, and prejudice are good things and should be practiced more often. Even extremists in the cultural debate are often simply trying to protect their group (though at the expense of others, if necessary). Few sane people, if given the opportunity to create an ideal society, would build in prejudice and discrimination. But that is not really the issue at stake. The relevant question is, how do we remove prejudice and discrimination from our society, since they are already here? The answers to that question are complex, but they begin with our understanding that what we have in common is far greater than anything that separates us.

IT'S A SMALL WORLD

Have you ever thought about the incredible number of interests, traits, emotions, and values that you share with almost all other human beings? Nearly all of us value freedom and independence, fret about how we look, worry over the welfare of those we care about, and desire to be respected and admired. We all seek happiness, try to avoid pain, need to be loved, and dream of being more than we are now.

While our moral beliefs seem personal and individual, there are many important ethical principles that are almost universal. Most world religions and ethical systems include the principle that you should act toward others the way that you would want them to act toward you. Many cultures place high value on the ethical virtues of personal responsibility, truthfulness, respect for others, loyalty, and helping others in need. When cultural groups do have different ethical value systems, it is usually not because they believe in totally different ethical principles, but because they prioritize the principles differently. One cultural group may believe that one's personal independence is more important than one's duty to others, while another cultural group puts duty to others first. Even beneath our differences are often important similarities.

WHAT DO YOU SEE?

Have you heard the old definitions of an optimist and a pessimist? An optimist sees a half glass of water as half full, while a pessimist argues that it is half empty. (See Illustration 9-2.) The content of the glass stays the same, the difference is in perception. Learning to live with cultural diversity works in a similar way. We can either choose to focus on what we have in common as human beings or on the factors that make us different. When you consider all of the things we share in common, the traits that make us different seem pretty insignificant.

> "It's only since World War II that human dignity became the focus of ethics; that we accepted the idea of an inviolable humanity regardless of race, culture, or whatever." (Darrell Fasching)

Illustration 9-2

CRITICAL THINKING

Here is your opportunity to think more carefully about factors that humans have in common with one another. Turn to Critical Thinking Exercise 9B on pages 157-158.

◼ Dealing With Our Differences

Of course, there are differences between people and between cultural groups. Our points of view are based partly on our experiences. Since different cultural groups have differing histories, their perspectives will differ as well. An effective strategy for dealing with cultural diversity will not ignore these differences, but use them in positive ways. But before that can happen people must face and conquer the greatest obstacle to unity and harmony—fear.

FEAR OF DIFFERENTNESS

"Without civic morality communities perish; without personal morality their survival has no value." (Bertrand Russell)

Fear is not wrong or bad in itself. In fact, fear is a natural form of protection possessed by most animals. Humans often interpret unfamiliar situations as threatening. Our bodies then produce additional amounts of the chemical adrenaline, increasing our alertness and awareness as well as our odds of surviving a dangerous situation. Inappropriate fear, then, is the real problem.

Tucked away deep in our subconscious minds is a little voice warning that every unfamiliar situation, person, habit, trait, belief, and characteristic represents a threat. Our rational minds know that this message is not true, but it influences us anyway. As a result, most people tend to feel more comfortable or safe around familiar things, people, and ideas. Some go a step further and believe that their safety and happiness depend on avoiding people who are different from them.

Two problems in this way of thinking become quickly apparent. One flaw is that, even though we share many common characteristics with others, each of us also has unique traits. No two people are exactly alike in every way. People who expend all of their energy avoiding differentness never learn how to live with others in the real world. Some sociologists and counselors point to this factor as one reason why so many American divorces occur during the early years of marriages. If you believe that two people have to be just alike for a relationship to last, then your relationships are not likely to last very long. The other flaw in avoiding people who are different is that differentness makes life more interesting. You may really enjoy macaroni and cheese (and feel very safe eating it), but it would be foolish to refuse ever to eat anything else. Variety really is the spice of life!

Differentness, then, is not something that we should automatically fear, but a tool that we can often use to the advantage of ourselves and our communities. One key to living in healthy, functional relationships with others is to learn to deal appropriately with differentness when it arises. Since the focus of this chapter is on cultural diversity, or the differences between cultural groups, we will now explore some strategies for effectively dealing with those differences. As you read the list, apply the critical thinking skills that you have been learning. Are there any of the strategies with which you disagree? Are there any strategies that you would add to the list?

Top 10 Strategies for Dealing Positively with Cultural Diversity

#10. *Keep a realistic perspective.* Until the Middle Ages, most humans thought that the earth was the center of the universe, with the sun, planets, and stars revolving around it. Of course, this belief was proven false when people learned more about the earth and the universe. There is a similar primitive human tendency to assume that one's cultural group is the center of the world ("normal") and that other cultural groups are odd or inferior. The key to overcoming this false assumption is to learn more about both your own cultural group and others.

#9. *Look for heroes everywhere.* Every cultural group has past and present heroes. One way to appreciate another culture is to find out about its heroes.

#8. *Keep learning.* Most hatred is based on fear, and most fear is based on ignorance. The more you learn about other cultures, the less you'll fear, and the more you'll appreciate others who are different. Knowledge evaporates fear.

#7. *Focus on similarities.* Remember that our similarities are greater than our differences. We have much more in common as human beings than what separates us as members of different cultures and subcultures.

#6. *Make a new friend.* The more people you know who are different from yourself, the less you will fear those differences. Make it a personal goal to make a new friend of another cultural group.

#5. *Practice empathy.* Empathy is the ability to understand and identify with another person's situation and feelings. It is a skill you can learn. Practice trying to see the world through the eyes of others. Attempt to understand and appreciate points of view that are different from your own.

#4. *Be fair.* Keep in mind that every culture has strengths and weaknesses. Intolerant people see only the strengths in their societies and the weaknesses in others. One sign of maturity is fairness, being able to recognize the strengths and weaknesses of your culture and those of others.

#3. *Learn from the past.* Cultures, like people, get their value systems from their experiences. To understand another culture, explore its history.

#2. *Avoid fallacies.* Rise above the fallacies of *hasty generalization* and *provincialism.* (See pages 66-67.) Don't assume that the negative actions of a few persons mean that everyone in their group is that way. Also, when conflicts and controversies arise between differing groups, try to understand each group's point of view.

#1. *Promote synergy.* Synergy means that some things are greater than the sum of their parts. Communities and societies are like that. Our differences combine to make us stronger. Just like a chorus needs singers with differing voices and an athletic team needs players with differing skills, America needs people with differing talents, interests, and points of view. After all, imagine how limited our society would be if everyone had the same mix of talents and abilities.

> "Only a life lived for others is a life worthwhile." (Albert Einstein)

> "No one can make you feel inferior without your consent." (Eleanor Roosevelt)

CRITICAL THINKING

To dig a little deeper into the issue of how people should handle differentness, complete Critical Thinking Exercise 9C on page 158.

■ So What Now?

"The greatest
friend of
Truth is Time,
her greatest
enemy is
Prejudice, and
her greatest
companion is
Humility."
(C. C. Colton)

Now that you better understand some of the difficult issues concerning cultural diversity, what will you do with what you have learned? After all, understanding a problem is not quite the same as helping to solve it. On issues such as discrimination and prejudice, each individual must choose whether to be part of the problem or part of the solution. And being part of the problem is not limited to those actively preaching hatred, intolerance, and division. In fact, many people who are part of the problem simply choose not to say or do anything at all when they witness injustice. Silence can be a form of approval.

You can be part of the solution by speaking out against prejudice when you see it. You can point out the fallacies in negative racial and cultural stereotypes. You can make a new friend from a different cultural group, or at least start by befriending someone who is different. You can get involved in school and community activities that bring differing groups of people closer together.

These steps may require courage. Some people find that as they open their minds and hearts to new friendships, old friends with closed hearts and minds turn their backs. But acting ethically often requires courage. The right action is not usually the easy action, at least at first. But remember that America, with all of its flaws, represents something wonderful to the world.

The founders of the United States dreamed of a place of equality where people from any race, religion, or ethnic group could find the freedom and the support to achieve their ambitions. No generation has yet fully lived up to that ideal, but many Americans throughout our history have worked and sacrificed to keep the dream alive. Every generation of Americans has the responsibility to keep working to make that dream come true.

CRITICAL THINKING

"I never met
a man I didn't
like."
(Will Rogers)

Critical Thinking Exercise 9D gives you an opportunity to apply your critical thinking skills to real-life problems related to cultural diversity. Turn to page 159.

Applications

1. **Write three things you have in common with all of your classmates.**

   _____

   _____

2. **Now write three ways that you are different from any of your classmates.**

   _____

   _____

3. **Which cultural group or subculture do you have the hardest time understanding and accepting? Why?**

   _____

   _____

4. **Journal.**

   a. **The most important thing I learned in this chapter was:**

   _____

   _____

   b. **One thing that I could do to be more accepting and tolerant of people different from me is:**

   _____

   _____

   c. **My favorite quotation from this chapter was (explain why):**

   _____

   _____

1. Explain two or three ways that you see each of the following American social values expressed in daily life in this country.

Critical Thinking Exercise 9A, Page 150

   a. All persons are created equal.

   _____

   _____

   b. All persons have equal rights to life, liberty, and the pursuit of happiness.

   _____

   _____

   c. Every voice—no matter what language it speaks—has a right to be heard.

   _____

   _____

   d. Unity does not come from uniformity, but from mutual respect and common interests.

   _____

   _____

2. List several examples of recent events in America that illustrate that discrimination and prejudice are still realities of life here.

   _____

   _____

   _____

   _____

List several specific examples of characteristics that most human beings have in common.

Critical Thinking Exercise 9B, Page 152

1. **Most human beings want, need, or seek:**

   _____

   _____

2. Most human beings fear or try to avoid:

_____

_____

3. Most human beings believe that:

_____

_____

4. Most human beings hope or dream that:

_____

_____

Critical Thinking Exercise 9C, Page 153

Answer the following questions about differentness _and how people should respond to it._

1. Which strategies from the Top 10 list did you think were the most helpful? Why?

_____

_____

_____

2. From your own experience, which strategies from the Top 10 list do you think are the most difficult? Why?

_____

_____

_____

2. From your own experience, what other strategies for dealing with cultural diversity would you recommend that were not on the Top 10 list? Why do you recommend them?

_____

_____

_____

ETHICS IN AMERICAN LIFE

Apply what you have learned about ethics, critical thinking, and cultural diversity to a real-world problem. Choose one example of a situation in your community or society in which different cultures or subcultures are clashing. Then use the Critical Thinking Model from Chapter 4 to find a better solution to the problem.

Step 1: Clearly state the ethical question under consideration.

_____

_____

_____

**Step 2: Research to find the information you need. Helpful
sources of information would probably include:**

_____

_____

_____

Step 3: Identify possible answers (solutions) to the question.

a. _____

b. _____

c. _____

d. _____

**Step 4: Evaluate the strengths and weaknesses of each
alternative.**

<u>Strengths</u>   **<u>Weaknesses</u>**

a. _____   _____

b. _____   _____

c. _____   _____

d. _____   _____

Step 5: Choose the best alternative and be able to defend it.

_____

_____

_____

1. On a small slip of paper, write one true and interesting fact about yourself that is unusual or unique. This fact could be a personal trait, characteristic, or even an experience. Write your name on the slip also. Then turn the slip in. Your teacher will mix the slips up and read them aloud, without revealing the names. Try to match which statements go with which of your classmates.

2. Write two or three examples of situations in which you have been discriminated against or have seen others being discriminated against. If you feel comfortable doing so, share these with your classmates and explain how experiencing or witnessing discrimination made you feel.

3. Write a short biography of a hero from a culture or subculture different from your own. Helpful sources of information could include encyclopedias or biographical books.

ETHICS AND THE
NATURAL WORLD

OBJECTIVES

After completing this chapter, you will be able to:

- 1. Identify ethical issues relevant to the relationship between people and the natural world.

- 2. Evaluate differing views regarding environmental ethics.

- 3. Identify ethical issues relevant to the treatment of animals by people.

- 4. Evaluate differing views that people have of animals and of animal ethics.

- 5. Apply critical thinking skills to ethical questions relevant to the natural world.

■ Focus

1. Describe what you think living conditions will be like for people, plants, and animals on planet earth in the year *3000*. Explain the reasons behind your predictions.

_____

_____

2. Who should receive most of the blame if the planet earth of the year 3000 turns out to be an environmental disaster? Why?

_____

_____

3. Who should be primarily responsible for cleaning up current environmental damages and preventing new ones? Why?

_____

_____

"He who knows what sweet virtues lie in the ground, the water, the air is a rich and noble man." (Ralph Waldo Emerson)

Have you noticed that many science-fiction stories and movies tend to portray the earth of the future as a barren, desolate planet? On the surface, the assumptions seem to be that either the future earth will be barely able to sustain life, or that humans will have given up and left for healthier planets. The deeper assumptions are that people are not taking very good care of their planet and will eventually pay dearly for this irresponsibility.

In this chapter you will explore some of the ethical issues at stake in the relationship between people and the natural world. You will evaluate differing points of view regarding these ethical issues. You will also apply critical thinking skills to difficult ethical questions related to human responsibilities, to the environment, and to animals.

■ Our Responsibilities Toward Planet Earth

Through astronomy, the study of the universe, humans have learned many valuable facts. Some of the most important lessons concern, ironically, not distant stars, but our own planet. (See Illustration 10-1.) We have discovered that the existence of life on earth is possible only because of a fragile balance of environmental conditions. Slight changes in global temperatures, air and water quality, or even plant populations have the potential to endanger the future welfare of the human species. What ethical responsibilities, if any, do we have to provide those future people with a pristine planet and a healthy quality of life?

Illustration

10-1

Environmental ethics is the field that seeks answers to moral questions concerning humanity's relationship with the natural world. Many of the issues studied in environmental ethics are probably not new to you. You have read and heard about such problems as water pollution, air pollution, global warming, ozone depletion in the atmosphere, overcrowded landfills, and the difficulties associated with safely disposing of hazardous wastes. Before you can fully understand these kinds of issues, you first must understand the complex ethical questions behind them.

ETHICAL QUESTIONS RELEVANT TO ENVIRONMENTALISM

In this section, you will focus on several key questions about environmental ethics. Look for strengths and weaknesses in the opposing arguments that follow each question.

1. *Do we have a moral responsibility to maintain a healthy environment on earth?*

NO. There is no real danger of the earth becoming uninhabitable in our lifetime. Only people in the distant future will suffer if the planet continues to deteriorate. We won't be here! Our generation did not create these environmental problems, so it is not our responsibility to fix them. If it makes some people happy to recycle and pick up trash, that's fine. But doing so isn't a moral or ethical responsibility. It is morally permissible to choose not to participate in environmental cleanup efforts.

YES. The problems are more dangerous and immediate than many people think. Many scientists believe that the dramatic increases in cancer rates in this century are caused primarily by environmental factors such as pollution. The deterioration of the ozone layer in the atmosphere is already causing near-epidemic levels of skin cancer in some countries. Huge segments of the world's population, some even in the United States, are facing serious shortages of safe drinking water. Our generation is partially responsible for the perilous condition of planet earth, and every person shares in the moral responsibility to help clean it up.

2. *If we don't act to clean up the environment, are we violating the rights of the earth or of future generations of people?*

NO. The *principle of rights* says that we have the right to do whatever we want to, as long as we don't violate the rights of another *person*. We can't violate the rights of planet earth, because planets don't have rights. Neither do people who may or may not exist in the distant future. Only actual living persons have rights that must be respected. Our only responsibilities are to take care of ourselves and to avoid harming other persons around us.

YES. It's true that the *principle of rights* allows for a lot of self-interest, but one moral principle cannot give us all of the answers to an issue this complex. Don't we owe people more than just not hurting them? The *principle of duties* contains an ethical concept called *universality*. It means that we should act like we would want others in the same situation to act. What if the roles were reversed and you were born in the year 3000? If you inherited dangerous living conditions that threatened your life and health, wouldn't you feel that the humans of the past had violated your rights?

3. *Do we have a moral responsibility to sacrifice our own comfort and convenience to benefit people of the future?*

NO. It's silly to argue that we have some kind of responsibility to potential people who aren't even alive and may never be! Why should we sacrifice our happiness, comfort, and convenience for people who don't yet exist? Every generation has to make the best of whatever kind of world it inherits. Our only responsibilities are to ourselves.

YES. Imagine what our quality of life would be like today if the people in generations before us had been totally self-centered! The progress of humans throughout history has happened largely because people were willing to look beyond their own self-interests to make a better world for those coming after them. It is terribly inconsistent to accept the comforts and benefits given to us by previous generations without trying to pass on similar benefits to others.

CRITICAL THINKING

Use Step 4 of the Critical Thinking Model (Chapter 4) to evaluate the strengths and weaknesses in the **YES** and **NO** arguments you just read. Turn to Critical Thinking Exercise 10A on pages 171-172.

IS COMMON SENSE ENVIRONMENTALISM POSSIBLE?

Extremists in the environmental debate sometimes make it sound as though there are only two options available to us. The *sacrifice the planet* extreme argues that we should continue to raise our standard of living at the expense of future generations. The *sacrifice ourselves* extreme maintains that we should deprive ourselves and suffer so that more resources will be left for our descendants. However, some people argue that the best answers may lie in *creative solutions* between the extremes. (See Illustration 10-2.)

**Illustration
10-2**

Sacrifice
the Planet
|——————————————|——————————————|
Search for
Creative Solutions

Sacrifice
Ourselves

For example, consider the issue of energy consumption and production. The sacrifice the planet view might argue that citizens in wealthier, developed nations, such as the United States, should feel free to consume as much energy as they can afford to produce. If producing that energy economically requires the use of fuels that could be environmentally harmful, such as oil and coal, so be it!

The sacrifice ourselves point of view might argue that environmentally harmful fuels should never be used, even if that means that people's consumption of energy is drastically limited. Creative solutions could include people not wasting energy, and all nations beginning to rely more on less-polluting energy sources such as solar power and wind.

CRITICAL THINKING

To analyze other environmental issues and problems, complete Critical Thinking Exercise 10B on pages 172-173.

■ Our Ethical Responsibilities to Animals

The relationship between humans and the natural world also includes ethical questions about how people should treat animals. How people view animals plays an important role in determining how they answer these questions. (See Illustration 10-3.)

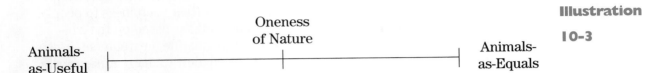

Oneness
of Nature

Animals-
as-Useful

Animals-
as-Equals

**Illustration
10-3**

THE ANIMALS-AS-USEFUL VIEW

One traditional view of animals has been to divide them into four categories: food, tools, pets, and threats. According to this *animals-as-useful* approach, an animal's worth is based only on its usefulness to people. Useful animals, such as cows (food, tools), horses (pets, tools), and dogs (pets, tools) are valued and protected. On the other hand, animals that are seen as useless or as threats to people are not only left unprotected, but at times are even slaughtered. As a result, many large predator species perceived by humans to be threats, such as bears, sharks, and tigers, are now in danger of extinction themselves.

This way of understanding nature and animals may have been necessary in previous generations, when people were still exploring and settling wilderness areas around the planet. At least for citizens of wealthier, developed nations, however, those days are long over. A conception of animals that once helped ensure our survival may now be threatening the future health of our planet.

THE ANIMALS-AS-EQUALS VIEW

At the opposite extreme from the animals-as-useful view is the *animals-as-equals* perspective. This approach maintains that all animals are equal in value and that humans are nothing more than a different species of animal. Since we assume that all people have equal rights, it is then logical to assume that all other animals are also entitled to those same equal rights. Proponents of the animals-as-equals view argue that *speciesism,* the belief that one species is superior to others, is just as wrong as *racism,* the belief that one race of people is superior to others. If one living creature has moral rights, they all do.

One chief problem with this approach has been consistency. It has been cynically referred to by some as the "Bambi and Thumper Ethic," since, even among animal rights advocates, cute animals sometimes seem to get more sympathy and attention. If bunnies, porpoises, and monkeys have rights, do roaches? Is it logical that some animals would have more rights than others? Also, as you have seen when trying to apply the principle of rights to human situations, granting rights to a being does not answer all of the questions. It still must be determined which rights are being granted. Do poisonous snakes have the same right to life that people have? Do termites have the same right you do to nest in your home? Do mosquitoes have a right to suck your blood? It is easy to see why even many animal activists are abandoning the principle of rights in arguing for the ethical treatment of animals.

> "I have all my life been a strong advocate for humanity to animals, and have done what I could in my writing to enforce this duty... but how many lives and what a fearful amount of suffering have been saved by the knowledge of parasitic worms through experiments... on living animals." (Charles Darwin)

> "I hold that the more helpless a creature, the more entitled it is to the protection of man from the cruelty of man." (Mahatma Gandhi)

THE ONENESS-OF-NATURE VIEW

A third way of looking at animals, the *oneness-of-nature* view, considers animals and humans to be parts of a larger **ecosystem**, or environmental network. The goal of this approach is not to conquer nature, but to maintain its balance and harmony. This view is not based on equality or superiority, but responsibility. Since humans are the most advanced creatures on earth, humans have the most responsibility to protect the ecosystem. In this oneness-of-nature perspective, animals have a worth and value that is independent of their usefulness to people. Sharks may still threaten people, but the worth of sharks is based on the irreplaceable role they play in maintaining balance in the marine environment.

While the oneness-of-nature view seems relatively new to many Americans and Europeans, it is really very old. The Greek philosopher, Aristotle, wrote about the unity and harmony of nature in the 4th century B.C. People in African, Asian, and Native American cultures have adopted this view of animals and nature for centuries. In many ways, humans around the world are now recognizing that the ancient oneness-of-nature tradition may represent the best hope for the future of life on earth.

CRITICAL THINKING

To further evaluate these three views of animals, complete Critical Thinking Exercise 10C on pages 174-175.

HOW SHOULD PEOPLE TREAT ANIMALS?

You have seen some of the reasons why this is not an easy question to answer. We are living in a transition period as far as how people perceive animals and the ethical treatment of animals. A decade or two ago, many "serious" scholars laughed at the idea of including animal-related issues in a discussion of ethics. However, that seems to be changing. Recent surveys have indicated that many people, especially teenagers and young adults, now regard these ethical issues as very high priorities.

As you have also seen, how people view animals has a lot to do with how they think animals should be treated. A person adopting the animals-as-equals viewpoint will usually end up with different conclusions than someone with the animals-as-useful perspective. These differences sometimes seem much greater than the ideas and principles that we hold in common. However, there may be a few basic guidelines about the ethical treatment of animals on which most people agree.

For instance, almost everyone would agree that intentional cruelty to animals is wrong. This is not a new idea. Immanuel Kant, the German philosopher of the 1700s, argued that humans have a basic moral duty to avoid acting cruelly to anyone or anything. He believed that people who treated animals with cruelty would develop a "cruel character." It is interesting to note that some recent studies of the lives of serial murderers have indicated that, as children, many of them did indeed torment and torture animals. Where disagreement arises about cruelty to animals is in defining what *cruel* means. Is it cruel to kill cows to make hamburgers and steaks? Is it cruel to use poison to keep your house free of rodents?

Another area of general agreement is that humans should avoid causing the extinction of animal species if at all possible. Every kind of animal and plant seems to have a specific role to play in the overall ecosystem. It is important to understand that not all extinctions of animal species are caused by human intervention.

The fossil record demonstrates that, regularly throughout history, some species have disappeared as new species arose to replace them. However, the development of human civilization with its cities, roads, industries, and pollutants has unnaturally speeded up the natural extinction process. Plant and animal species are now disappearing much faster than they can be naturally replaced. As a result, many biologists warn that the diversity of life on earth is being thinned out at an alarming rate. With each missing link, the chain of life is further weakened.

CRITICAL THINKING

Apply the Critical Thinking Model to an animal ethics case study. Turn to Critical Thinking Exercise 10D on pages 175-176.

Remember, this section is reserved for your personal ideas, opinions, and feelings. You will not be required to turn in or share these responses with others.

1. Place an X on the continuum below to show where you think your attitude about the environment was *before* you studied this chapter. Then place an O to show where you think it is now. In the spaces following the continuum, explain why you put the marks where you did.

Sacrifice the planet for our needs

Find creative solutions to meet our needs and those of future people

Sacrifice ourselves to help future people live better

_____

_____

_____

2. Place an X on the continuum below to show what your view of animals was *before* you studied this chapter. Then place an O to show what you think it is now. In the spaces following the continuum, explain why you put the marks where you did.

Animals-as-useful

Oneness-of-nature

Animals-as-equals

_____

_____

_____

3. Journal.

a. **One of the most important things I learned in this chapter was:**

_____

_____

b. **One thing that I will try to do to help protect the environment is:**

_____

_____

c. **My favorite quotation from this chapter was (explain why):**

_____

_____

Evaluate the strengths and weaknesses of the YES and NO arguments given in the text. Then, in #4, create your own YES and NO arguments that relate to the question you are given.

1. Do we have a moral responsibility to maintain a healthy environment on earth?

NO ARGUMENTS

Strengths   **Weaknesses**

_____   _____

_____   _____

YES ARGUMENTS

Strengths   **Weaknesses**

_____   _____

_____   _____

2. If we don't act to clean up the environment, are we violating the rights of the earth or of future generations of people?

NO ARGUMENTS

Strengths   **Weaknesses**

_____   _____

_____   _____

YES ARGUMENTS

Strengths   **Weaknesses**

_____   _____

_____   _____

3. Do we have a moral responsibility to sacrifice our own comfort and convenience to benefit people of the future?

NO ARGUMENTS

Strengths   **Weaknesses**

_____   _____

_____   _____

YES ARGUMENTS

Strengths   **Weaknesses**

_____   _____

_____   _____

4. **Create your own YES and NO arguments: Should protecting the environment have a higher priority than business profit and providing jobs for people today?**

NO ARGUMENTS

_____

_____

_____

YES ARGUMENTS

_____

_____

_____

Critical Thinking Exercise 10B, Page 164

For each of the following environmental issues, give one example of what people at the sacrifice the planet *extreme and people at the* sacrifice ourselves *extreme might suggest should be done. Then write what you think represents a creative alternative to the extremes.*

1. **The shortage of safe drinking water in many parts of the world**

The *sacrifice the planet* approach might say:

_____

_____

The *sacrifice ourselves* approach might say:

_____

_____

One example of a creative solution would be:

_____

_____

  2. Overcrowded landfills and other problems associated with garbage and waste disposal.

The _sacrifice the planet_ approach might say:

_____

_____

The _sacrifice ourselves_ approach might say:

_____

_____

One example of a creative solution would be:

_____

_____

  3. The damage done to the ozone layer in the atmosphere by the use of gasoline-powered automobiles

The _sacrifice the planet_ approach might say:

_____

_____

The _sacrifice ourselves_ approach might say:

_____

_____

One example of a creative solution would be:

_____

_____

Describe what you think each of the views of animals would say about the morality of the following actions.

1. Commercial whaling

The *animals-as-useful* view:

_____

_____

The *animals-as-equals* view:

_____

_____

The *oneness-of-nature* view:

_____

_____

2. Destroying animal habitats by building and developing in wilderness areas and rain forests

The *animals-as-useful* view:

_____

_____

The *animals-as-equals* view:

_____

_____

The *oneness-of-nature* view:

_____

_____

3. Write your own controversial ethical issue related to the treatment of animals by people. Then explain the different points of view as you did in Questions #1 and #2.

_____

_____

_____

The *animals-as-useful* view:

_____

_____

The *animals-as-equals* view:

_____

_____

The *oneness-of-nature* view:

_____

_____

_____

Critical
Thinking
Exercise
10D,
PAGE 167

Carefully read the following case study. Then, based on the ideas that you have learned in this chapter, give arguments that could be used for and against the experiment. Evaluate the strengths and weaknesses of both sets of arguments.

THE CASE OF THE DROWNING OF THE DOGS

The Public Health Department at Mythical State University is pioneering a research program to find new drugs that will save the lives of more drowning victims. Resuscitating victims through traditional CPR methods often has serious drawbacks. Many times it doesn't work at all and, even when it does, victims are often left with serious brain damage caused by lack of oxygen. Several drugs designed to reduce this brain damage look promising, but need to be tested on living subjects.

Since there are serious ethical problems with using human subjects in such experiments, the scientists want to use animals. Large dogs have been chosen for the experiment because their heart and lung systems are similar to those of humans. The plan is to intentionally drown about 30 of the dogs and then to compare the success rates of resuscitating them with and without the new drugs. It is hoped that the drugs will save more dogs and reduce the occurrence of brain damage.

Somehow, word of the project was leaked to the media. Several animal rights groups are now angrily protesting against the proposed experiments. They are pointing out that many of the dogs will die terrifying and horrible deaths, and that even many of the survivors will have to be destroyed after the tests because of injuries. They also argue that, unlike humans, the dogs cannot understand what is being done to them, and thus cannot participate voluntarily.

The scientists and doctors agree that at least half of the 30 dogs will die or have to be destroyed. But they argue that if this experiment is successful, the new drugs could save *thousands* of human lives. They add that they have learned all that they can about the drugs from computer models and experiments on mice. Using the dogs is absolutely necessary before the drugs can be administered to people. Should this experiment be done?

1. Arguments for the Experiment

_____

_____

2. Arguments Against the Experiment

_____

_____

3. Strengths and Weaknesses of the FOR arguments:

Strengths   **Weaknesses**

_____   _____

_____   _____

4. Strengths and Weaknesses of the AGAINST arguments:

Strengths   **Weaknesses**

_____   _____

_____   _____

1. Write a research paper about one controversial issue or problem relevant to environmental ethics. Your teacher can help you choose a topic. Use the following steps from the Critical Thinking Model:

Step 1—Clearly state the ethical question under consideration.

Step 2—Research to find the information you need.

Step 3—Identify possible answers to the question.

Step 4—Evaluate the strengths and weaknesses of each alternative.

Step 5—Choose the best alternative and be able to defend it.

2. As a class, choose a current environmental issue or problem in your area. Learn more about the issue through library research, guest speakers, a field trip, or surveys of people in the community. After gathering your research, discuss differing views about the issue and what else should be done to address the problem.

3. Write your own definitions for the following important concepts that were discussed in the text. What do they mean to you?

   a. Environmental ethics:

   _____

   _____

   b. The *sacrifice the planet* view of environmentalism:

   _____

   _____

   c. The *sacrifice ourselves* view of environmentalism:

   _____

   _____

   d. Ecosystem:

   _____

   _____

CHAPTER 10 Ethics and the Natural World   **177**

e. The *animals-as-useful* view:

_____

_____

f. The *animals-as-equals* view:

_____

_____

f. The *oneness-of-nature* view:

_____

_____

ETHICS IN ENTERTAINMENT

OBJECTIVES

After completing this chapter, you will be able to:

■ 1.   Identify ethical issues relevant to entertainment.

■ 2.   Define censorship.

■ 3.   Describe and illustrate legal principles upon which censorship laws are often based.

■ 4.   Apply critical thinking skills to develop a system of entertainment self-guidance.

■ Focus

The entertainment industry often uses surveys to determine the opinions of its audiences. The following is a survey to test your opinions about ethical issues in entertainment.

ENTERTAINMENT OPINION SURVEY

Indicate your level of agreement or disagreement with each of the following statements by circling the appropriate words. Then briefly explain the reasons behind your responses.

1. There is too much emphasis on violence in American entertainment.

STRONGLY AGREE   **SOMEWHAT AGREE**   **SOMEWHAT DISAGREE**   **STRONGLY DISAGREE**

_____

_____

2. There is too much emphasis on sex in American entertainment.

STRONGLY AGREE	SOMEWHAT AGREE	SOMEWHAT DISAGREE	STRONGLY DISAGREE

_____

_____

3. People's actions are affected by the kinds of entertainment that they watch, listen to, and read.

STRONGLY AGREE	SOMEWHAT AGREE	SOMEWHAT DISAGREE	STRONGLY DISAGREE

_____

_____

4. Those responsible for including so much sex and violence in American entertainment are not trying to influence our social values, but are merely reflecting the values already present in our society.

STRONGLY AGREE	SOMEWHAT AGREE	SOMEWHAT DISAGREE	STRONGLY DISAGREE

_____

_____

ON SECOND THOUGHT

Since ethical issues and questions seem to exist in every facet of life, it should not seem surprising that we find them in the area of entertainment. In this chapter, you will investigate some of those issues. You will also explore the legal principles behind the laws that limit some forms of entertainment. Finally, you will learn specific strategies that can help you make more mature and responsible personal decisions about the kinds of entertainment you choose to enjoy.

■ Ethical Issues in Entertainment

Talking about ethics in entertainment makes some people uncomfortable. After all, entertainment is about personal tastes and preferences. Ethics is about rules and principles of morality. Thus, some people fear that combining the two will inevitably lead to some groups trying to impose their tastes and preferences on other groups. There are certainly groups trying to do that in America today.

However, refusing even to discuss or consider ethical issues in entertainment is an overreaction. Only by talking about difficult problems and by sharing our mutual concerns can we begin to find better answers. The forms of entertainment we enjoy raise many difficult ethical issues that demand our thoughtful attention.

VIOLENCE IN ENTERTAINMENT

Much of American entertainment is violent. You have probably seen or heard some of the statistics. It has been reported that, before turning 18 years of age, American children witness an estimated 180,000 acts of violence on television alone. Is it just a coincidence that violent crime rates in America are among the highest in the world? Studies with young children have consistently shown a connection between watching violence and acting violently and aggressively toward others. Whether the same effect also occurs with teenagers and adults has not been as well-established.

"I sometimes think the media has dreamed our history up." (Oliver Stone)

SEXUAL CONTENT IN ENTERTAINMENT

Complaints about the sexual content in song lyrics, movies, and television shows probably outnumber even the complaints about violence. One factor behind the complaints is that sexual themes are so pervasive. The entertainment industry has learned that sex sells. It sells movie tickets, music albums, books, magazines, and, through advertising, almost everything else.

"A life without festivities is like a road with no end." (Democratus, 400 BC)

Another complaint is that sex in entertainment is not portrayed accurately or responsibly. The message we see so often is that love and sex are the same thing, or at least that you cannot have one without the other. Movie and television lovers always seem to have perfect bodies, perfect teeth, and perfect hair. They seem to remind the rest of us how imperfect we are. Movie and television lovers rarely worry about protecting themselves from AIDS and other sexually transmitted diseases. They rarely use birth control, yet they rarely have unwanted pregnancies. Critics charge that such naive and romanticized portrayals of sex are both irresponsible and dangerous.

OBJECTIONABLE LANGUAGE IN ENTERTAINMENT

The language used in our entertainment has become offensive to many people. Words that were once banned in movie theaters can now be heard on prime time television shows and even in children's movies. Young children find themselves confused by the discrepancy between the language standards demanded by their parents and teachers and those used by many of their heroes in sports and entertainment. Television shows, movies, popular music concerts, sporting events, and celebrity interviews are now peppered with words and phrases that make many teenagers and adults uncomfortable.

CRITICAL THINKING

To further analyze these ethical issues in entertainment, complete Critical Thinking Exercise 11A on pages 191-192.

Controlling Entertainment Through Laws

Censorship refers to actions taken by authority figures to suppress materials that are considered objectionable or to restrict people's abilities to read, view, or listen to such materials. In the technical definition of censorship, the authority figures referred to are representatives of the government. However, in a looser sense, school officials, librarians, television station managers, and parents can also censor materials.

Some people argue that government authorities should use censorship laws to ensure that only wholesome, inoffensive forms of entertainment are allowed. Others argue that the United States Constitution forbids the passing of such laws. One key to making sense of this debate over censorship is understanding the legal principles underlying all governmental laws. Just as moral decisions are based on ethical principles, decisions to pass laws are based on *principles of legislation.* These principles are used to justify why laws prohibiting certain behaviors should be passed.

THE PRINCIPLES OF LEGISLATION

The **harm principle** states that actions that cause *harm to others* can be legally prohibited. (See Illustration 11-1.) Most violent crime laws fall into this category. For example, the laws prohibiting murder, rape, and assault are based on the harm principle. However, the meaning of the harm principle is not limited only to *physical* harm. Laws against stealing and fraud prevent *financial* harm. Those banning child neglect protect people from *emotional* or *psychological* harm.

Illustration

11-1

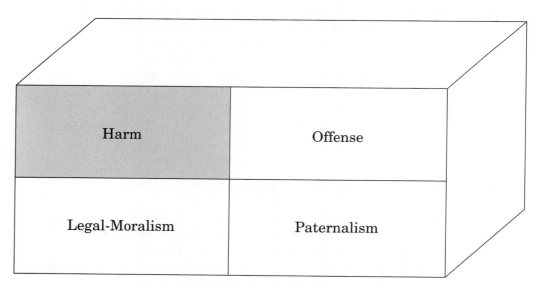

Principles of Legislation

The **offense principle** states that actions that cause *offense to others* can be legally prohibited. (See Illustration 11-2.) In a sense, offending people is seen as a milder version of harming them. A practical problem, of course, is that different people are offended by different things. However, when enough people are

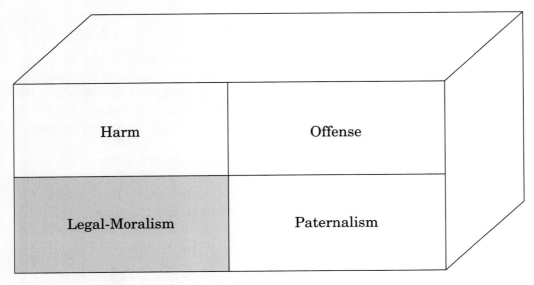

Harm | Offense

Legal-Moralism | Paternalism

Principles of Legislation

Illustration 11-2

offended by the same type of behavior, laws are sometimes passed to prohibit that behavior. Laws banning public nudity, obscene language on radio and television stations, and "hate speech" are based on the offense principle.

The **legal-moralism principle** states that actions that are considered *morally wrong* can be legally prohibited. (See Illustration 11-3.) With this principle, there is no need to demonstrate that people are harmed or offended, only that the actions in question are morally wrong. Again, people do not always agree on which actions are morally wrong. However, laws prohibiting prostitution, homosexual behavior, and, in some places, the operation of certain businesses on Sundays are based on the legal-moralism principle.

"You can tell the ideals of a nation by its television advertisements." (Norman Douglas)

Harm | Offense

Legal-Moralism | Paternalism

Principles of Legislation

Illustration 11-3

The **paternalism principle** states that actions that would cause people to *harm themselves* can be legally prohibited. (See Illustration 11-4.) The word *paternal* means fatherly or parent-like. Thus, laws based on paternalism imply that the government has taken on the parental responsibility of protecting people from harming themselves. Laws prohibiting suicide, the personal use of dangerous drugs, and driving a car without wearing a seat belt are based on the paternalism principle.

Illustration

11-4

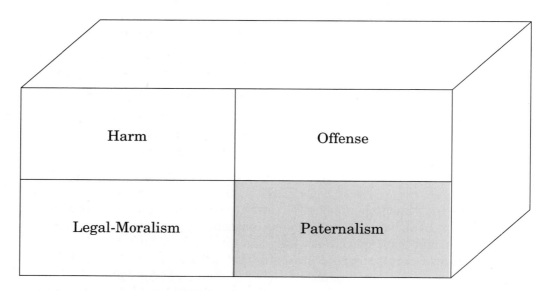

Principles of Legislation

CRITICAL THINKING

To see how well you understand the four principles of legislation, complete Critical Thinking Exercises 11B and 11C on pages 192-194.

APPLYING THE CONSTITUTION TO CENSORSHIP LAWS

You are probably wondering how all of these legal matters apply to the issue of censorship in entertainment. Well, American laws can be passed by city, county, state, and federal government officials. However, only laws that do not violate the terms of the United States Constitution can be upheld as valid and enforceable. The courts, and ultimately the Supreme Court, determine whether laws exceed constitutional limits.

The First Amendment's guarantee of freedom of speech is a strong argument against censorship laws. "Congress shall make no law . . . abridging the freedom of speech, or of the press . . ." The intent of the Constitution is clear. People should be legally free to say and write what they want. The authors of the Constitution knew that people would occasionally find some speech offensive, or even believe it to be morally wrong. But that fact alone does not outweigh the value of freedom of speech.

On the other hand, all rights have limits. The *principle of rights,* the foundation of the Constitution, makes it clear that in exercising your rights, you may not violate the rights of other people. A classic example is that your right to free speech does not include the right to shout "Fire" in a crowded theater. Such an irresponsible act would likely cause injury and death to people. Similarly, if a strong case can be made that the production of a book, magazine, or film causes actual harm to people in society, then the government's authority to ban that material is increased. Thus, the censorship laws most likely to stand up to constitutional scrutiny are those based on the *harm principle*.

On the other hand, censorship laws based on the *offense principle* or the *legal-moralism principle* are more likely to be judged as unconstitutional. Some legal scholars argue that these laws represent the very type of government interference that the First Amendment was designed to prevent.

Censorship laws based on *paternalism* are intended to restrict people from hearing, seeing, or reading things that could harm them. The First Amendment seems to imply, however, that adults should generally be able to make their own decisions about taking such risks. Paternalistic laws that limit the forms of entertainment that can be viewed by children are less likely to be overturned on constitutional grounds.

Perhaps now you can see why most people are neither totally for nor totally against censorship. We are, after all, talking about a conflict between two fundamental aspects of human nature—the need for limits versus the desire to test those limits. The issue is better understood as a continuum or spectrum across which differing points of view are spread. (See Illustration 11-5.) One end of the spectrum represents total censorship, meaning that any materials found to be even mildly offensive by anyone should be banned. Needless to say, that would not leave very much for us to read or watch. The other end of the spectrum represents a total ban on any censorship. Even child pornography, in which the harm caused to children is so obvious, could be legally produced, distributed, and purchased. Thus, most people's opinions on censorship probably lie somewhere in between the two extremes.

> "Every free man has an undoubted right to lay what sentiments he pleases before the public; to forbid this is to destroy freedom of the press; but if he publishes what is improper, mischievous, or illegal, he must take the consequences." (Sir William Blackstone)

Where Are You?

Total Censorship •————————————————————• No Censorship

Illustration 11-5

CRITICAL THINKING

Here is your chance to apply what you have learned about controlling entertainment through censorship laws. Turn to Critical Thinking Exercise 11D on page 194.

■ Developing Self-Guidance in Entertainment

If government censorship is not the most effective strategy in setting higher standards for entertainment, then what is? For young children, the solution probably lies in parents becoming more aware and more involved in their children's entertainment habits. However, for teenagers only a few years away from adulthood and independence, the more appropriate alternative is to develop the habit of self-guidance, or personal responsibility.

WHY BOTHER?

There are several reasons why developing self-guidance is worth the trouble. First, having high personal standards concerning the entertainment you choose is a sign, and possibly even a source, of maturity. Adults—parents, teachers, and bosses—are likely to notice this maturity and reward you with additional independence, authority, and responsibility. After all, trust and respect are earned, not given.

A second, related reason for learning self-guidance is that rights carry with them obligations and responsibilities. Compared to many other people in the world, Americans have tremendous personal freedom. This freedom is guaranteed by the Constitution. However, when people abuse that freedom through irresponsible actions, authorities often respond by clamping down and limiting individual rights. You can probably remember several incidents from your childhood in which your own irresponsible actions led your parents to take away some of your privileges. The rights to free speech and choices in entertainment carry with them the responsibility to use those rights wisely.

Finally, practicing self-guidance in entertainment is one method of developing a healthy mental lifestyle. "Garbage in—garbage out" is a maxim or saying among computer programmers. It means that, if you are careless about the instructions you give to a computer, you should not be surprised if the results are not to your liking. It is not hard to see the logic in applying that maxim to the human mind. What we think, how we think, and perhaps even how we act are influenced greatly by the information we enter into our mental computers. If you want to have a healthy, physically fit body, you must set high standards as to what you put into your body. In the same way, if you want to have a healthy and fit mind, you must set high standards as to what you put into your mind.

HOW TO DEVELOP SELF-GUIDANCE IN ENTERTAINMENT

There are several practical steps you can take to become more selective about the entertainment you enjoy. One positive strategy is to think of your time as something you *invest*, not just something you spend. When you are watching a program or listening to a tape or CD, ask yourself, is this really worth my time? What am I getting out of this? The concept of investing your time does not mean that you can only watch stuffy, serious shows and movies from now on. Laughter is a vitally important part of emotionally healthy living. However, it does mean that you begin to see entertainment more as a tool to meet your needs and less as a way of wasting time.

Another good strategy is to learn to analyze how different forms of entertainment make you feel. Once you tune in to your feelings, you will probably find that some forms of entertainment consistently make you feel stressed, tense, or depressed. Others may leave you feeling happy, relaxed, and peaceful. You might also consider how different forms of entertainment make you feel about other people. Do some types of entertainment often make you feel irritable and angry? Is that how you want to feel?

A third strategy to developing self-guidance is to apply the critical thinking skills you have been learning to your entertainment experiences. This means

ETHICS IN AMERICAN LIFE

becoming a *smart shopper* of entertainment. (After all, think about how much money you will spend on entertainment this year!) Practice the skill of reading between the lines to analyze what you are watching, reading, or listening to. What are the artists, directors, and writers trying to say? Why are they saying it this way? Do you agree with them? How would you say it differently?

Choosing the path of self-guidance in entertainment requires more than a little courage. This is a decision to think for yourself, to break away from the herd. You may find that some forms of entertainment that your friends still enjoy are just not worth your time, at least not all the time. Not all teenagers can overcome the fear of separating themselves from the group. Those that do, however, often find themselves leading the group.

Along the way, you may also be surprised to find that your parents are becoming your allies. Their respect and admiration for you is likely to grow as they see you taking more personal responsibility and making mature entertainment decisions. Your parents will probably not always agree with all of your entertainment choices and decisions. However, by demonstrating that you are acting and thinking maturely, you are increasing the likelihood that they will trust your judgment.

> "Two roads diverged in a wood, and I— I took the one less traveled by, and that has made all the difference." (Robert Frost)

Applications

As in previous chapters, this section is reserved for your personal thoughts, opinions, and feelings. You will not be required to turn these answers in or share them with others.

I. **One example of a censorship law that I believe is right and appropriate is:**

_____

_____

_____

2. **One example of a censorship law that I believe violates the First Amendment guarantee of free speech is:**

_____

_____

_____

3. **Personalize each of the strategies for developing self-guidance in entertainment. Write one specific way that you could implement each strategy into your life.**

a. **Think of your time as something you *invest*, not just something you spend.**

_____

_____

_____

b. **Analyze how different forms of entertainment make you feel.**

_____

_____

_____

c. **Apply the critical thinking skills you have been learning to your entertainment experiences.**

_____

_____

_____

4. Journal.

    a. **One concept or idea that I learned in this chapter is:**

    _____

    _____

    b. **When I analyze my personal entertainment habits, the strengths I see are:**

    _____

    _____

    c. **When I analyze my personal entertainment habits, the weaknesses I see are:**

    _____

    _____

Briefly explain how each of the following ethical principles might apply to the ethical issues described in your text. (To review the principles, see pages 21–28 in Chapter 2.)

Critical Thinking Exercise 11A, Page 181

1. Is the emphasis on violence in American entertainment wrong?

a. **The principle of egoism** _____

_____

b. **The principle of utility** _____

_____

c. **The principle of virtues** _____

_____

d. **The principle of rights** _____

_____

e. **The principle of duties** _____

_____

2. Is the emphasis on sex in American entertainment wrong?

a. **The principle of egoism** _____

_____

b. **The principle of utility** _____

_____

c. **The principle of virtues** _____

_____

d. **The principle of rights** _____

_____

e. **The principle of duties** _____

_____

3. Is the emphasis on objectionable language in American entertainment wrong?

   a. The principle of egoism _____

   _____

   b. The principle of utility _____

   _____

   c. The principle of virtues _____

   _____

   d. The principle of rights _____

   _____

   e. The principle of duties _____

   _____

Critical Thinking Exercise 11B, Page 184

Explain which principle of legislation serves as the basis for each of the following laws and why.

   1. **This law requires all motorcycle riders to wear helmets.**

   _____

   _____

   2. **This law forbids certain obscene words from being broadcast by television and radio stations.**

   _____

   _____

   3. **This law prohibits close relatives from marrying each other or having sexual relations.**

   _____

   _____

ETHICS IN AMERICAN LIFE

4. This law forbids the consumption of alcoholic beverages by minors.

_____

_____

5. This law prohibits arson.

_____

_____

6. This law forbids certain "indecent" styles of swimsuits from being worn on public beaches.

_____

_____

7. This law prohibits individuals from selling illegal drugs, such as cocaine and heroin.

_____

_____

8. This law forbids the sale or purchase of alcoholic beverages on Sunday mornings.

_____

_____

Give two original examples of laws based on each of the legal principles discussed in the text. (These do not necessarily have to be valid laws where you live. You can make up any laws you wish.)

Critical Thinking Exercise 11C, Page 184

The harm principle:

1. _____

2. _____

The offense principle:

1. _____

2. _____

The legal-moralism principle:

1. _____

2. _____

The paternalism principle:

1. _____

2. _____

Create one original censorship law based on each of the legal principles discussed in the text. Then explain whether or not you think your example violates the First Amendment guarantee of freedom of speech. (These do not necessarily have to be valid laws where you live. You can make up any laws you like.)

The harm principle:

Law: _____

Explanation: _____

_____

The offense principle:

Law: _____

Explanation: _____

_____

The legal-moralism principle:

Law: _____

Explanation: _____

_____

The paternalism principle:

Law: _____

Explanation: _____

_____

1. Divide into small groups of 3 to 5 students each. Make a list of recent television shows, movies, and popular songs that included the ethical issues discussed in this chapter (violence, sexual content, objectionable language, and censorship). Share your examples with your classmates, then discuss which issues seem to be the most common. Which issues do people seem to get the most upset about? Why do you think that is?

2. Apply the Critical Thinking Model from Chapter 4 to an ethical issue relevant to entertainment. You can use one of the issues mentioned in the text of this chapter or choose a different one in which you are interested. Remember that an ethical issue is one that involves the concepts of moral right and wrong.

Step 1: Clearly state the ethical question under consideration.

_____

_____

Step 2: Research to find the information you need. (List possible sources of information here.)

_____

_____

_____

_____

Step 3: Identify possible answers to the question.

a. _____

b. _____

c. _____

d. _____

Step 4: Evaluate the strengths and weaknesses of each alternative, relying especially on ethical principles and fallacies.

<u>Strengths</u>	<u>Weaknesses</u>
a. _____	_____
b. _____	_____
c. _____	_____
d. _____	_____

Step 5: Choose the best alternative and be able to defend it. Give your "best answer" here and give the main reasons why you chose it over the other alternatives.

_____

_____

_____

_____

3. Survey some of the people you know who have lived in other countries, or who are from different cultural groups than you are. How is ethics in entertainment viewed differently by these different groups?

_____

_____

_____

_____

4. Read the following quotation from Plato's *Republic*. Then write down your reactions to the passage. What could the implications be for censorship laws in America? With what parts do you agree? Disagree? Why?

You know that the beginning is the most important part of any work, especially in the case of a young and tender thing; for that is the time at which the character is being formed and the desired impression is more readily taken. . . . Shall we just carelessly allow children to hear any casual tales which may be devised by casual persons, and to receive into their minds ideas for the most part the very opposite of those which we would wish them to have when they are grown up? We cannot. . . . Anything received into the mind at that age is likely to become indelible and unalterable; and therefore it is most important that the tales which the young first hear should be models of virtuous thought. (Source: William J. Bennett, The Book of Virtues, New York: Simon & Schuster, 1993.)

_____

_____

_____

_____

_____

5. Write your own definitions for the following important concepts that were discussed in the text. Paraphrase, using your own words. What do the concepts mean to you?

a. Censorship _____

_____

_____

b. The harm principle _____

_____

_____

c. The offense principle _____

_____

_____

d. The legal-moralism principle _____

_____

_____

e. The paternalism principle _____

_____

_____

f. The First Amendment guarantee of freedom of speech _____

_____

_____

g. Self-guidance in entertainment _____

_____

_____

ETHICS AND HUMAN SEXUALITY

OBJECTIVES

After completing this chapter, you will be able to:

■ 1. Define sexual ethics.

■ 2. Analyze various explanations of the purposes of human sexuality.

■ 3. Describe and evaluate philosophies relevant to human sexuality.

■ 4. Apply critical thinking skills to current controversies relevant to sexual ethics.

■ Focus

Sexual ethics is the branch of ethics in which people attempt to find the best possible answers to moral questions about human sexuality. These real-life questions are often personal and complex. The following exercise will introduce you to some of these ethical questions.

DARLA'S DILEMMA

Darla is one of your good friends. Recently, she found her first true love, Jake, and has been spending a lot of time with him. The two of them are almost always together at school, usually arm-in-arm, holding hands, or kissing. One Saturday morning Darla calls you at home. She is upset and wants to ask your opinion about some things. The following are Darla's questions. What would you tell her?

Note: These questions call for some rather personal responses on your part. You will not be required to share your answers with others if doing so would make you feel uncomfortable.

1. "Jake is telling me that if I really loved him I would want to make love. I don't feel like I'm ready to do that yet. What should I say or do?"

_____

_____

_____

2. "I'm afraid that if I don't agree to have sex with Jake that he will leave me and look for somebody else. Should I give in to keep him?"

_____

_____

_____

3. "When we kiss a lot, I can tell that Jake gets aroused. He has told me that he is afraid he will get so excited that he won't be able to control himself. Can that really happen?"

_____

_____

_____

Before trying to wrestle with the morality of sexual behaviors, you first must address basic questions about the purpose of sex. As you will see, however, your view of the purpose of sexual intercourse has a lot to do with how you view the morality of specific sexual actions.

■ The Purposes of Human Sexuality

The Greek philosopher, Aristotle, argued that moral right and wrong are based, at least in part, on the purpose of things. His approach works well in studying sexual ethics. To understand the morality of sexual behaviors we need to first understand the purpose of human sexual intercourse. What is sex for? It may sound like a simple question, but the implications of the possible answers are important.

REPRODUCTION

One purpose of intercourse is reproduction, sometimes referred to as _procreation_. This is, as far as we know, the only purpose of sexual intercourse for animals. That fact is significant because Aristotle believed that many of the purposes of things could be found in the patterns and laws of nature. So, according to this view, reproduction is the only purpose of sexual intercourse in nature, and people are part of nature. Therefore, reproduction is the only appropriate purpose of sexual intercourse for people.

The sex-for-reproduction view has interesting implications. (See Illustration 12-1.) If the only purpose of sex is reproduction, then using birth control would be self-defeating. Romantic love would not be considered wrong, but could be seen as unnecessary. **Monogamy**, the custom of having one sexual partner or mate for life, would not be necessary to reproduce, but might be viewed as important to the welfare of the children that would come along.

PURPOSES OF SEXUAL INTERCOURSE

Illustration

12-1

	Reproduction	Intimacy	Pleasure
Birth control	Illogical	Encouraged	Encouraged
Romantic love	Not necessary, but encouraged to promote family unity	Important	Not necessary
Monogamy	Not necessary	Important	Probably discouraged

The Implications of Different Potential
Purposes of Sexual Intercourse

The critics of the sex-for-reproduction view argue that sexual behaviors are controlled by instinct to a much greater degree in animals than in people. These critics assert that our greater freedom from instinct and our ability to reason creatively give us more choices as to the purposes of sex. In other words, reproduction is obviously *a* purpose of sexual intercourse, but it may not be the *only* purpose, or even the *primary* purpose.

INTIMACY

A second possible purpose of sexual intercourse is intimacy. In philosophical terms, intercourse is said to have unitive significance. **Unitive significance** refers to the powerful ability that sex has to unite people, to bring them closer together. Indeed, we speak of sex as causing two people to become one, not just physically, but emotionally as well.

"The basic discovery about any people is the discovery of the relationship between its men and its women." (Pearl S. Buck)

The implications of sex-for-intimacy are different from the implications of sex-for-reproduction. Birth control, seen as an obstacle to reproduction, has an important role if the primary purpose of sex is intimacy. Advocates of birth control argue that closeness and unity actually increase when couples can make love without fearing that pregnancy will result. Also, romantic love plays a more important role in sex-for-intimacy. Love for a partner is not required to have a baby, but it is an important factor in the development of intimacy. Monogamy, though not necessary for intimacy, might be encouraged. After all, it takes a long time for intimacy to develop between people.

The primary critics of the sex-for-intimacy view are the people who believe that the main purpose of sex is reproduction. They argue that the concepts of romance and intimacy are fairly recent inventions in human history. Intimacy may be nice, they say, but people were having sex and babies long before people thought of romance and intimacy.

PLEASURE

A third potential purpose of sexual intercourse is pleasure. According to supporters of this view, because sex can cause intense physical pleasure, pleasure should be seen as the primary purpose of sex. The sex-for-pleasure view has its own set of implications. Birth control is encouraged, since it allows for pleasurable experiences without the complications of pregnancy. Romantic love and monogamy would likely be seen as unnecessary, and possibly even as complicating factors. Love, intimacy, and commitment tie you to one person, possibly causing you to miss out on pleasurable experiences with others.

Critics of the sex-for-pleasure view agree that pleasure is a natural consequence of sex. However, they argue that this fact does not prove that pleasure is the *primary* purpose of sexual intercourse. After all, rubbing your skin lightly with a feather results in the natural consequence of feeling tickled. However, the primary purpose of feathers is causing birds to fly, not tickling people.

It probably seems obvious to you that sexual intercourse could have more than one purpose. However, even if all three purposes are valid, they still must be prioritized. Which one is the most important purpose? Which one ranks second? Third? Carefully thinking through this ranking for yourself is important, because the implications of each potential purpose are so different.

CRITICAL THINKING

To further consider the purposes of sexuality for humans, complete Critical Thinking Exercise 12A on page 211.

> "Tyranny grows from a lack of self-control. Our passions forge our chains."
> (Jean-Jacques Rousseau)

■ Philosophies of Sexual Ethics

Understanding something of the purpose of sexuality does not answer all of our questions. How do we decide which sexual behaviors are morally right and which are morally wrong—or even whether terms like *morally right* and *morally wrong* can be applied to sex? Our next step is to consider several different philosophies of sexual ethics, or different ways of thinking about sexual morality. These philosophies are not limited only to American thinking. In fact, they can be found in many different cultures and nations. However, each philosophy is a part of America's past or present sexual ethical value system.

THE OLD DOUBLE STANDARD

The old double standard refers to the belief that males and females should have different sexual moral rules. This view of sexual ethics seems to have been predominant in America a few decades ago. It has diminished recently, but has not completely disappeared. The philosophy implies that it is usually acceptable for males to engage in sexual intercourse, but not for females. Thus, sex becomes an activity enjoyed by *all* males, but only by *bad* females. *Good* females are expected to remain virginal and chaste until marriage.

The old double standard assumes that the purpose of sexual intercourse for males is pleasure. (See Illustration 12-2.) However, it assumes that the purpose of sex for females is to have children and build intimacy in marriage. This two-tiered system of moral rules can lead to dishonest, manipulative situations. Males could resort to offering love to get sex, while females might be tempted to offer sex in hopes of getting love. Relationships that begin on such an insincere foundation often have a hard time developing the honesty, intimacy, trust, and long-term stability for which most people are looking.

> "There is no pillow as soft as a clear conscience." (French proverb)

Purpose of Sex	The Old Double Standard	If It Feels Good Do It	As Long As We Love Each Other	Not Until We're Married
	Males ——— Pleasure ·········· Females ——— Reproduction and Intimacy	P L E A S U R E	Intimacy and/or Pleasure	Reproduction, Intimacy, and/or Pleasure

Illustration 12-2

Philosophies of Sexual Ethics and Purposes of Sexual Intercourse

IF IT FEELS GOOD, DO IT

If it feels good, do it is the view that virtually all sexual behaviors are morally acceptable. This view is based on a philosophical doctrine called hedonism. **Hedonism** is the assumption that all pleasure is inherently good. If pleasure is always good, then anything that produces pleasure must also be good. Sex produces pleasure, so sex is good. Pleasure is not only the purpose of sex, it is what makes sex morally right.

The *if it feels good, do it* philosophy came into prominence in America in the 1960s and 1970s. Women were growing more concerned about the unfairness of *the old double standard* and were speaking out against it. Ethical questions raised by the seemingly endless war in Vietnam, as well as other national and world events, led younger Americans to reconsider many of the traditional moral beliefs they had been taught. It was only natural that rules of sexual morality would be included. Sexual *promiscuity*, meaning having sexual relations with many different people, became morally permissible. More sex = more pleasure = more good. The "Sexual Revolution" was on!

Many critics of the *if it feels good, do it* philosophy are also critical of *the old double standard.* They argue that the primary purposes of sex are really reproduction and intimacy, and that the wrong change took place in the 1960s and 1970s. The women were wrong, they say, to adopt the traditional male view that the main purpose of sex is pleasure. It should have been the men who changed.

AS LONG AS WE LOVE EACH OTHER

During the 1980s, Americans seemed to start moving away from the *if it feels good, do it* philosophy toward a view that says that sex is permissible as long as the people involved love each other. The **as long as we love each other** philosophy states that sexual behavior is morally permissible if it is based on romantic love. According to this view, the main purposes of sexual intercourse are intimacy and pleasure, in that order.

Several factors are responsible for the social change to a more romanticized view of sexuality, but the major force has been AIDS. Sexually transmitted diseases (STDs), such as syphilis and gonorrhea, have existed for centuries, and were common during America's sexual revolution. However, by the 1960s and 1970s these diseases could usually be cured with penicillin. AIDS represents a much more terrifying threat. It is almost always fatal and there is, as yet, no cure on the horizon of medical research. People are learning that sexual promiscuity is, at least for now, not in their long-term best interests. Sexual safety now seems to be found in long-term, monogamous relationships.

Some critics charge that the *as long as we love each other* philosophy has problems of its own. Many of us "fall in love" with several different people in our lifetimes. If we have sexual relations with each person we love, and if each of them has also fallen in love with several others before, we could still be exposing ourselves to AIDS and other sexually transmitted diseases. That is the main reason why many health experts strongly recommend that protective measures, such as condoms, be used every time people participate in sexual intercourse, even if it is within a loving, monogamous relationship.

NOT UNTIL WE'RE MARRIED

Sometimes teenagers wrongly assume that everyone around them is already sexually active. This is not true. It is also not true that teenagers who are not sexually active are old-fashioned or suffering from social problems. Many high school students, college students, and even young adults are now choosing to adopt a lifestyle of abstinence.

Abstinence refers to a personal decision to avoid participation in sexual intercourse for a certain period of time. There are several valid reasons why people might choose to abstain from sexual relations until they get married. For one thing, people who are not sexually active are much less likely to be exposed to

AIDS and other sexually transmitted diseases. The AIDS epidemic is still spreading rapidly around the world. And in America today, the fastest growing group of new AIDS victims are young heterosexuals.

Some young people choose to abstain from sexual relations because of their religious beliefs. Others commit to abstinence because participation in sex carries with it emotional and psychological baggage that they do not yet feel ready to face. Whatever the reasons behind the choice, abstinence is not a decision that anyone should have to feel embarrassed about.

CRITICAL THINKING

To reinforce what you have learned about the philosophies of sexual ethics, turn to pages 212-214 and complete Critical Thinking Exercises 12B and 12C.

■ Current Controversies in Sexual Ethics

Today's American high school students and young adults are facing many important sexual ethics issues. Each of these issues poses unique problems for people who are trying to live ethical lives. Three of those issues, sexual harassment, date rape, and homosexuality, will be discussed in this section.

SEXUAL HARASSMENT

Sexual harassment is the act of using sex to dominate, control, or debase another person. The term also refers to the practice of using one's personal power in a relationship to obtain sexual favors from another. Until just a few years ago, sexual harassment was one of America's dirty little secrets. People knew that it happened, but nobody talked about it. However, several recent scandals and allegations of scandals have brought the issue into the open. Among those publicly accused of sexual harassment have been nationally known figures in government, education, the courts, business, entertainment, the military, sports, and even religion.

Sexual harassment presents some unique problems for society. Some people have found that being accused of sexual harassment was enough to ruin their reputations and careers, even if the charges were untrue. In most other crimes, people are assumed to be innocent until proven guilty. With sexual harassment, however, people are sometimes placed in the impossible position of trying to prove their innocence. How can anyone prove that something did not happen? If he says one thing happened while she claims something else, whom should we believe?

The fact that sexual harassment is difficult to prove should never be taken to mean that the act is acceptable. Sexually harassing others violates almost all of the ethical principles that we have discussed in this study. On top of everything else, it represents an abuse of power. When bosses use their positions to harass employees, or when teachers use their positions to harass students, they are misusing the authority that they have been given.

> "I regard sex as the central problem of life . . . Sex lies at the root of life, and we can never learn to reverence life until we know how to understand sex."
> (Henry Ellis)

DATE RAPE

Date rape is the act of forcing or coercing a friend or acquaintance to participate in sexual activities without his or her consent. Until recent years, it was another of America's dirty little sexual secrets. Date rape, or acquaintance rape, is now recognized as the most frequent type of rape in our society.

In the past, women, the primary victims of date rape, were often too afraid or embarrassed to tell anyone what had happened. The victims often felt, or were even told, that the rape was their fault. They had somehow led the man on, or encouraged him in some way. Many people believed that men, once sexually aroused, could not control themselves or be responsible for their actions.

The predicament of women became even more impossible when some people combined this myth about men with the philosophy of *the old double standard*. The resulting attitude was that "good girls" were expected to use their sexuality to attract males, but were not allowed to participate in sexual intercourse. Since these people believed that males were unable to control themselves, the female became responsible for controlling both herself and her date. Such people believed, however, that she should do so in a way that would keep him interested in her. What kind of "wonder woman" could accomplish all of that?

A dating system like this is not fair to males, either. To be told that you are not capable of controlling your sexual urges is to be told that you are an animal instead of a man. It is dehumanizing. As human beings, we are not totally controlled by sexual instincts. We are rational and free; therefore, we are responsible for our actions. We cannot expect others to respect us, or be able to respect ourselves, if we believe that we have no control over our actions. The national attention being given to date rape may lead us to carefully evaluate many of our assumptions about the relationships between men and women. If so, the result could be more responsible, equal, and honest relationships for us all.

HOMOSEXUALITY

Homosexuality refers to having sexual desire for persons of one's own gender, or participating in sexual activities with a person of one's own gender. This is in contrast to the term **heterosexuality**, which refers to having sexual desire for persons of the opposite gender, or participating in sexual activities with a person of the opposite gender. While the morality of homosexuality has been hotly debated in America in recent years, it is anything but a new phenomenon. References to homosexuality can be found in ancient writings from many different nations and cultures.

Some people believe that all homosexual acts are morally wrong. Several reasons are often given in defense of this view. First, many religions have doctrines, beliefs, and traditions that condemn homosexual actions. Secondly, it is often argued that homosexual acts are unnatural. This contention is most likely to be raised by those who subscribe to the sex-for-reproduction view discussed earlier. They maintain that, since homosexual acts cannot lead to reproduction, then only heterosexual intercourse is appropriate. An underlying assumption of these attitudes toward homosexuality is that people are not *born* as homosexuals or heterosexuals, but make a voluntary *choice* to follow one lifestyle or the other.

Other people contend that homosexual acts are not morally different from heterosexual acts. These people argue that homosexuality does not, in itself, violate the principles that we use to make any other ethical decisions. Some religious groups, furthermore, are changing and adapting their beliefs to allow more flexibility about people's sexual orientations. This view maintains that the primary purposes of sexual intercourse are intimacy and pleasure, which are possible in both heterosexual and homosexual relationships. An underlying assumption of these attitudes toward homosexuality is that each person is born with either a heterosexual or a homosexual orientation. Supporters of these beliefs say that homosexuality is not a matter of voluntary choice; it is just the way you are.

CRITICAL THINKING

Critical Thinking Exercise 12D gives you an opportunity to apply the Critical Thinking Model from Chapter 4 to one of the sexual ethics issues mentioned in the preceding section, or to another sexual ethics issue in which you are interested. Turn to page 214 for more details.

Applications

As in previous chapters, this section is reserved for your personal thoughts and opinions. You will not be asked to turn in these answers or share them with others.

1. **How would you describe the purpose or purposes of human sexuality? If you think there is more than one purpose, how would you prioritize or rank them?**

   _____

   _____

   _____

2. **Which of the philosophies of sexual ethics seems the closest to the sexual value system you want to have? Which seems to be the most opposed to your personal sexual value system? Why?**

Closest _____

   _____

   _____

   _____

Most opposed _____

   _____

   _____

   _____

3. **Write a brief opinion concerning each of the following controversies in sexual ethics. Do you tend to think of this action as morally right, morally wrong, or as not being a moral issue? Why?**

   a. **Sexual Harassment**

   _____

   _____

   _____

   b. **Date Rape**

   _____

   _____

   _____

c. Homosexuality

_____

_____

_____

4. Journal.

Write a letter to yourself explaining your personal convictions about sexual ethics and defining your sexual values. What is moral sexual behavior to you? Why?

Dear _____ **,**

_____

_____

_____

_____

_____

_____

_____

_____

_____

_____

_____

Write a paragraph explaining each of the potential purposes of sexual intercourse. Include differences that you would expect to result in people's attitudes about sex and in their sexual behaviors.

Reproduction

_____

_____

_____

_____

_____

_____

Intimacy

_____

_____

_____

_____

_____

_____

Pleasure

_____

_____

_____

_____

_____

_____

_____

Write a paragraph explaining each of the philosophies of sexual ethics. What sexual attitudes and behaviors would you expect to see in people who follow each philosophy?

Males Following the Old Double Standard

_____

_____

_____

_____

_____

Females Following the Old Double Standard

_____

_____

_____

_____

_____

_____

If It Feels Good, Do It

_____

_____

_____

_____

_____

_____

As Long As We Love Each Other

_____

_____

_____

_____

_____

_____

Not Until We're Married

_____

_____

_____

_____

_____

_____

_____

List what you consider to be strengths and weaknesses of each of the following philosophies of sexual ethics.

The Old Double Standard

Critical Thinking Exercise 12C Page 205

<u>**Strengths**</u>   <u>**Weaknesses**</u>

_____   _____

_____   _____

_____   _____

_____   _____

If It Feels Good, Do It

Strengths   **Weaknesses**

_____   _____

_____   _____

_____   _____

_____   _____

As Long As We Love Each Other

Strengths   **Weaknesses**

_____   _____

_____   _____

_____   _____

_____   _____

Not Until We're Married

Strengths   **Weaknesses**

_____   _____

_____   _____

_____   _____

_____   _____

Critical Thinking Exercise 12D Page 207

Apply the Critical Thinking Model (Chapter 4) to one *of the current controversies in sexual ethics.*

Step 1: Clearly state the ethical question under consideration.

_____

_____

Step 2: Research to find the information you need. Helpful sources of information would probably include:

_____

_____

_____

Step 3: Identify possible answers (solutions) to the question.

a. _____

b. _____

c. _____

d. _____

Step 4: Evaluate the strengths and weaknesses of each alternative, focusing on ethical principles and fallacies.

<u>Strengths</u>   <u>Weaknesses</u>

a. _____   _____

b. _____   _____

c. _____   _____

d. _____   _____

Step 5: Choose the best alternative and be able to defend it.

_____

_____

_____

_____

1. **Create a survey form to learn more about people's attitudes about sex. You will be asking for personal information, so be very careful to protect everyone's privacy. Ask for people's opinions about the purpose of sex, sexual harassment, date rape, homosexuality, etc. Look for trends and patterns when analyzing the responses you get. Do males view the purpose of sex differently than females? Does age make a difference in one's opinions about sexual harassment?**

2. **Conduct a media scavenger hunt for stories and articles related to sexual ethics. Collect newspaper and magazine articles, and watch for examples of sexual ethics issues in television shows, movies, and music. Combine your findings with those of your classmates. Discuss together what kinds of sexual messages our society is sending us. Are these messages realistic? Do you agree with them?**

3. Conduct research to find out how people in different nations and cultures think about sex. What do they perceive the purpose of sex to be? What other differences can you discover? Your research could include library sources, but also try to find people from different cultures and nations to interview.

GLOSSARY

Abstinence: a personal decision to avoid participation in sexual intercourse for a certain period of time. (p. 204)

Active euthanasia: a situation in which a suffering person is intentionally killed. (p. 133)

Animals-as-equals view: the approach which maintains that all animals are equal in value and that humans are nothing more than a different species of animal. (p. 165)

Animals-as-useful view: the approach which maintains that an animal's worth is based only on its usefulness to people. (p. 165)

As long as we love each other: the philosophy which states that sexual behavior is morally permissible if it based on romantic love. (p. 204)

Assumption: a belief, stated as a fact, that cannot be proven true or false. (p. 83)

Authority: a source of ethical beliefs which states that the morality of an action is right or wrong because "someone said so." (p. 5)

Balancing needs: an understanding of morally mature people that living a complete life means meeting your own needs and those of others. (p. 50)

Benefits: features that companies might not be ethically required to provide for their workers, but offer anyway to attract high quality employees. (p. 85)

Bioethics: the study of ethical issues related to medicine and health. (p. 132)

Business ethics: the branch of ethics in which people attempt to apply moral principles to workplace questions. (p. 82)

Censorship: refers to actions taken by authority figures to suppress materials that are considered objectionable or to restrict people's abilities to read, view, or listen to such materials. (p. 182)

Citizen-leaders: individuals who are actively involved in the process of government. (p. 103)

Code of ethics: a written set of ethical guidelines that workers are expected to follow. (p. 83)

Computer viruses: programs that are designed to damage or negatively affect other computers, usually by causing the loss of information. (p. 119)

Concordance: agreement or harmony. (p. 44)

Conflict of interest: a situation where people who have agreed to act in the best interests of others choose to act in their own interests instead. (p. 86)

Consequences: the effects or results of what we do. (p. 21)

Critical thinking: a problem-solving process based on the use of reason, creativity, and consistent thinking. (p. 63)

Cultural diversity: the fact that the world is comprised of many distinct and unique ethnic, racial, and religious groups. (p. 148)

Culture: a source of ethical beliefs which states that the morality of an action depends upon the beliefs of one's culture or nation. (p. 5)

Date rape: the act of forcing or coercing a friend or acquaintance to participate in sexual activities without his or her consent. (p. 206)

Duty: an ethical obligation that one individual has to others. (p. 27)

Ecosystem: environmental network. (p. 166)

Egoism principle: the idea that the right thing for a person to do in any situation is the action that best serves that person's own long-term interests. (p. 22)

Either/or: the fallacy of making it appear that there are only two possible sides to an issue, one good and one bad. (p. 65)

Empathy: the skill of understanding the feelings and perspectives of others. (p. 67)

Employee duties: the ethical obligations that employees have to their employers. (p. 85)

Employee rights: those things that workers are owed by their employers. (p. 85)

Environmental ethics: the field that seeks answers to moral questions concerning humanity's relationship with the natural world. (p. 163)

Ethical principles: general statements of how people should or should not act in most situations. (p. 3)

Ethical system: the way in which an individual, group, or subculture decides which actions are moral and which are immoral. (p. 21)

Ethics: the field of philosophy that studies the morality of human conduct. (p. 4)

Euthanasia: killing that is done in the victim's best interests, usually to relieve intense suffering. (p. 133)

Fallacies: inappropriate or deceptive arguments. (p. 64)

False appeal to authority: the fallacy of incorrectly relying on authority figures or experts to back up your argument. (p. 67)

False appeal to popularity: the fallacy of assuming that an idea is right because many people believe that it is. (p. 68)

Genes: microscopic parts of chromosomes which influence the inheritance and development of specific characteristics. (p. 136)

Genetic engineering: the process of creating genes that serve specific purposes. (p. 137)

Genocide: the annihilation of racial, political, or cultural groups. (p. 150)

Government ethics: the branch of ethics in which people attempt to apply moral principles to the ethical questions arising in public service. (p. 98)

Hacking: the act of using one's own computer equipment to "break into" the computer system of others and find information. (p. 119)

Harm principle: the principle which states actions that cause harm to others can be legally prohibited. (p. 182)

Hasty generalization: the fallacy of assuming that most members of a group share a common characteristic, when this assumption is actually based on only a few observations. (p. 66)

Hedonism: the assumption that all pleasure is inherently good. (p. 203)

Heterosexuality: refers to the sexual desire for persons of the opposite gender or participating in sexual activities with a person of the opposite gender. (p. 206)

Homosexuality: refers to the sexual desire for persons of one's own gender, or participating in sexual activities with a person of one's own gender. (p. 206)

If it feels good, do it: the view that virtually all sexual behaviors are morally acceptable. (p. 203)

Inconsistency: a fallacy of contradicting ourselves in words or actions without being able to explain the changes. (p. 65)

Innate: referring to that which is somehow built into us rather than taught. (p. 41)

Internet: massive worldwide web of connected computers. (p. 120)

Intuition: a source of ethical beliefs which states that the morality of an action is dependent upon the principles of right and wrong that have been built into one's conscience. (p. 6)

Is/ought: the fallacy of stating that, because things are a certain way now, that must be how they should be. (p. 66)

Justice: impartial fairness or equity. (p. 41)

Legal-moralism principle: the principle which states actions that are considered morally wrong can be legally prohibited. (p. 183)

Living wills: a document which clearly states a person's wishes regarding life-sustaining medical procedures. (p. 135)

Martyr syndrome: the mistaken belief that seeing yourself as a "good person" requires having to sacrifice yourself or your needs for others. (p. 50)

Materialism: an excessive concern for possessions and wealth. (p. 105)

Monogamy: the custom of having one sexual partner or mate for life. (p. 201)

Moral development: the process of growing more ethically mature. (p. 41)

Moral duty: an ethical obligation that one individual has to others. (p. 85)

Morality: the part of human behavior that can be evaluated in terms of right and wrong. (p. 4)

Networks: complex systems of computers connected by modems and high-speed telephone lines. (p. 120)

Nonvoluntary euthanasia: a situation in which an individual is not mentally capable of deciding what he or she wants. (p. 133)

Offense principle: the principle which states actions that cause offense to others can be legally prohibited. (p. 182)

Old double standard: the belief that males and females should have different sexual moral rules. (p. 203)

Oneness-of-nature view: the approach which considers animals and humans to be parts of a larger ecosystem, or environmental network. (p. 166)

Others-centeredness: a characteristic of people who ignore their own needs and interests to meet the needs of others . (p. 49)

Passive euthanasia: a situation in which the victim is not killed, but merely allowed to die by withholding medical treatments. (p. 133)

Paternalism principle: the principle which states actions that would cause people to harm themselves can be legally prohibited. (p. 184)

Post hoc: the fallacy of assuming that, because two events happened in a short period of time, the first action must have caused the second one. (p. 66)

Procreation: one purpose of sexual intercourse which is reproduction. (p. 200)

Provincialism: the fallacy of looking at an issue or question only from your point of view, or the point of view of people like you. (p. 67)

Questionable claim: the fallacy of using statements that are too broad or too exaggerated to be true. (p. 67)

Racism: the belief that one race of people is superior to others. (p. 165)

Reason: a source of ethical beliefs which states that the morality of an action is based on consistent, logical thinking. (p. 6)

Red herring: the fallacy of using an unrelated idea in an argument to distract your opponent. (p. 66)

Respect for persons: the principle which states that it is always wrong to use other people in ways that harm them for your own benefit. (p. 27)

Right: how an individual is entitled to be treated by others. (p. 26)

Sacrifice the planet: an extreme theory which argues that society should continue to raise its standard of living at the expense of future generations. (p. 164)

Sacrifice ourselves: an extreme which maintains that society should deprive themselves and suffer so that more resources will be left for our descendants. (p. 164)

Self-centeredness: a characteristic of people who are only interested in meeting their own needs and interests. (p. 49)

Sexual ethics: the branch of ethics in which people attempt to find the best possible answers to moral questions about human sexuality. (p. 199)

Sexual harassment: the act of using sex to dominate, control, or debase another person; the practice of using one's personal power in a relationship to obtain sexual favors from another. (p. 205)

Slippery slope: a fallacy where one attempts to frighten others into rejecting an idea by trying to show that accepting it would start a chain reaction of terrible events. (p. 67)

Social contract: a higher moral authority which represents the deepest values and beliefs of a society. (p. 46)

Software piracy: the act of making many copies of a disk and then selling the copies for much less than the software's retail price. (p. 118)

Speciesism: the belief that one species is superior to others. (p. 165)

Standard: an accepted level of behavior to which persons are expected to conform. (p. 6)

Standard of ethics: social expectations of people's moral behavior. (p. 7)

Standard of etiquette: expectations concerning manners or social graces. (p. 7)

Standard of law: rules of behavior imposed on people by governments. (p. 7)

Two-wrongs-make-a-right: the fallacy of defending something that you did wrong by pointing out that someone else did it, too. (p. 65)

Unitive significance: the powerful ability which sex has to unite people, to bring them closer together. (p. 201)

Universality: the idea that you should act as you would want others to act in the same situation. (p. 27)

Utility principle: the idea that the morally right action is the one that produces the best consequences for everyone involved, not just for one individual. (p. 23)

Virtue: an ideal character trait that people should try to incorporate into their lives, or a trait commonly found in morally mature people. (p. 24)

Voluntary euthanasia: a situation which requires that a victim be mentally competent and desire to die. (p. 133)

Whistle-blowing: the act of reporting unethical or illegal actions by one's superiors or peers to authorities or to the media. (p. 87)

INDEX